ENDOR‹

—✕

"This book is extremely insightful on what the Bible says the last days will look like. William does an excellent job of showing the parallels of the condition of the world in the days of Noah and the troubles we see unfolding today. The great news is, we don't have to be afraid because of the salvation provided by Jesus Christ. Praise the Lord all the answers we need are available to us in His Word."
— Kimberly Jimenez,
disciple of Jesus and insurance agent
Tucson, AZ

"It is with great pleasure that I give to you an endorsement for your newest book *Spiritual Warfare*. From one author and friend to another, *kudos* to you! You have tackled what most men and women tend to avoid. *Spiritual Warfare* is a book that is needed greatly among brothers and sisters in the faith; it is so vital for today. I thank you so much for this book with its thought-provoking questions and spiritual guidance."
In His grip and grace,
— Shirley Katz, author of the upcoming book,
Life from the Dead!
Jacksonville, FL

"*As of the Days of Noah* gives us a powerful insight in the days we are living. William Chandler brings it alive with God's written Word in a way everyone can understand."

—Richard A. Garcia, government employee
Tucson, AZ

"A great book for those seeking to understand what the future has to hold! The author takes an in-depth look at what Scripture reveals about our present condition in relation to 'the days of Noah.' The book is a great read that ultimately reveals God's glorious plan for mankind!"

—Ray and Christy McCraw
Tucson, AZ (UOfA graduates, retired,
and living by the grace of and in the service
of our Lord Jesus Christ daily!)

"Blessings to you, William. May your book touch the hearts and minds of those who read it and bring about a new understanding of God's plan from before the beginning of time!"

"Have you noticed how much the times have changed? Commercials today that would have never been allowed five to ten years ago? Our children and our families are inundated by the media. There are cultural and social changes that can somewhat be shocking. This book inspires us to seek answers in the Word of God and to trust and rest in Jesus."

—Patricia L. Guillen, Front Office Coordinator
Tucson, Arizona

SPIRITUAL WARFARE
AS THE DAYS OF NOAH

WILLIAM E. CHANDLER

SPIRITUAL WARFARE
AS THE DAYS OF NOAH

XULON PRESS ELITE

Xulon Press
2301 Lucien Way #415
Maitland, FL 32751
407.339.4217
www.xulonpress.com

All Scripture is taken from the King James Version Cambridge Bible, 1769.

The Greek and Hebrew from the Strong's Blue letter Concordance to the Bible.

The Young's Analytical Concordance to the Bible.

The New Unger's Bible Dictionary

Many other sources also are provided near the quotations.

Printed in the United States of America.

ISBN-13: 978-1-54567-942-5

Acknowledgments

—๛—

This is my fifth book. I cannot begin to tell you how humbled and grateful I am to God my Father, and His Son Jesus Christ, my Lord, to be on this journey, and for the sacrifice He made, and the invitation to become His child through the New Birth experience in the spirit; otherwise, none of this would have been written.

I'm not the only author, as you perfectly know, yet in God's wisdom He has placed each of us in His plan by laying upon our hearts to serve him.

No matter how we see ourselves (in our eyes), He will work with us as we work together with Him. He uses the whole church that we might grow and learn, and for that, I'm extremely thankful.

I have seen brothers that I knew personally go home to see Jesus, and others are still here.

Pastors alive now, and those in glory, have influenced me with their love, kindness, truth, wisdom, knowledge, correction, instruction, and encouragement over the years, to take each day "one day at a time," and to seek after His will, not my own.

To have these men and women in my life added to my faith.

I give double honor to those who labor in the written Word of God.

I would like to acknowledge with gratitude and blessings my friend and brother in Christ, Doug Priore, for his assistance in reading my manuscript and his grammar suggestions. He is also a fellow author of the books, *Brainwashed* and *Jurassic Park and the Bible*, plus he is writing the foreword to this book, which I'm sure you will enjoy.

To all my family and dear friends in Christ, you have been a blessing in this world more than you will ever know.

I would like to honor my wife, best friend, companion, and fellow worker in Christ, Sheri, who has stayed beside me through thick and thin. She has encouraged me, and has been that scriptural wife (Eph. 4:2; 1 Pet. 4:8; Prov. 18:22, 31:10–31).

May all those who read this book be blessed, and then study those things, which they read. The world will become more evil than we ever imagined, yet in Christ Jesus we can have peace, rest, and confidence. Sharing the true answer, Jesus, can change your life.

Blessings in the name of Jesus.

Contents

---㎿---

FOREWORD

—⁀ɯ⁀—

Prepare to be blessed and prepare to be challenged—and instructed—by what the scriptures teach, as revealed in this new book by William Chandler.

People over the years have understood and taught various ideas about the Nephilim (giants) as mentioned in the Bible. William Chandler delves into this topic in considerable detail, and some of what he uncovers and shares within these pages may come as a surprise (as it sometimes did to me), *especially* as it relates to the biblical concept of "kinds." Certain ideas may go counter to what you previously have imagined and believed, but stay with him. This is an important subject in need of clarification, and Mr. Chandler has much to offer in this dialogue.

He also speaks in detail about the abilities of men in the days of Noah. If you have accepted the concept that man developed slowly over many thousands of years, and that centuries ago man was rather primitive, then you have been deceived. In the past few decades, discoveries have been made that loudly proclaim that man was much more advanced in ages past than we have been led to believe. The book of Genesis documents that men lived to great ages in times past, and this allowed for men to develop their capabilities perhaps even beyond what we see today, and many of those early advancements have only recently been rediscovered today. As the book of Ecclesiastes informs us, "There is nothing new under the sun." Man lived to great ages and enjoyed enhanced potential either to serve God or to serve Satan. Likewise, just as each person in ages past had to choose, so today, each person must also choose whom he will serve.

Scripture verses are woven generously throughout the text, so that the conversation continually aligns with God's thoughts. You will be entertained with descriptions of what life possibly was like for Noah and for those people alive during that period of history, even though actual written records have been lost, having been lost during the flood of Noah.

William also has much to say in his typical conversational style on the subject of rebellion, since it was rebellion against God in the days that Noah lived that caused God to bring the flood upon the earth. There is increasing rebellion in children as the generations advance in our current times. As expected, Mr. Chandler has sound biblical advice on this problem as well, and as we near the time of Jesus' return, Satan has amped up his influence it seems. Many aspects of Satan's influence are described within these pages.

We, as Christians, must continually remember that the spiritual warfare against us will never cease; we will be constantly under attack until Jesus establishes his 1000–year reign on Earth—a time we are eagerly awaiting.

Doug Priore
Author of two published books relating to the Bible, pastor of a small Christian church in Tucson Arizona, adjunct chemistry instructor at local community college, former service technician and dispatcher at gas utility company, served three years in the Peace Corps as high school instructor (in the Fiji Is.), proud father of son and daughter

(both in their 30's), and a lover of Jesus Christ and his creation, about which I thoroughly enjoy reading and studying.

THE CONFLICT

There was war in Heaven; swords were drawn, and met with impact as powers were being shaken. The storm was fiercely struggling for superiority.

The battle was already lost before it started. Yet with prideful intentions, the powers resisted with vigor. The fury of determination and desperation was vanquished; there was no contest.

"The powers fell, *as lightning from the atmosphere striking the earth,* being stripped of their angelic beauty, strength and former positions." (Luke 10:18)

> With rage, Lucifer cursed, as he felt the last of his angelic light draining from him. No longer would he be called beautiful, anointed, an angel of light, but an angel of darkness, never to be known as beautiful again, to receive the wages he had earned as the accuser, liar, deceiver, serpent, dragon, the destroyer, and the devil. The one who was once light lead astray a great number of angels to be chained in darkness and reserved for ultimate destruction. They would be called the prince and powers of the air (atmosphere). (Eph. 1:21–23; 2:2)

1

We would see Lucifer's influence upon man, through temptations to draw man further into wickedness and rebellion.

This is a part of Satan's nature: pride, rebellion (Isa. 14:12–15), hate, and revenge to work within humans and to inspire man's inventions while making him think he invented them (Ps. 115:4–8); to make man proud of the accomplishments by the works of his hands (Gen. 4:3).

God had a plan before the foundation of the world because he foresaw this. He would provide a savior, for he knew all men would fall; all would be sinners (Rev. 13:8; Isa. 59:12–16).

Satan lost peace and rest, and all pure things were defeated. Satan was filled with anger and spitefulness.

The book of Peter describes him perfectly:

"Be sober, be vigilant; because your adversary the devil, as a roaring lion, walketh about, seeking whom he may devour: Whom resist steadfast in the faith, knowing that the same afflictions are accomplished in your brethren that are in the world." (1 Peter 5:8–9)

God wants us to resist Satan by faith (steadfastness). He wants us to stand, trust, and believe on his promises; to believe God, knowing that what you are going through, others have also faced in their life. We are not alone; it is an honor and a reward to stand as our other brothers in Christ did before us.

Adam was formed, and God created life in him by his spirit. He made Eve also from one of Adam's ribs.

Adam was commanded of God to freely eat of all the trees, except one: the tree of the knowledge of good and evil.

The knowledge of which God spoke would give man an understanding of good and evil. As we study this command that God gave, we will see how it relates to the days of Noah.

Satan was blind with hate; he was only thinking of getting back at God by going after his creation. He heard when God said, "I will make man in my image." God also gave

Adam authority over the earth. Satan hated this, for wasn't he once the anointed cherub in heaven, as he tried to justify himself.

Satan might have said these words: "What should I do? Should I directly attack these humans to turn from God? Or should I use the skills which are assumptions, lies, doubt, confusion, speculation, and manipulation to appear as an angel of light?"

He said, "I will humor them. I will appeal to their nature. I will use trickery and deceit to draw them away from God. I will appease them in their minds and cause them to think it's all about themselves; to question, but not to deny God's words. I will be a friend to pride, achievement, advancement, and reputation, and to comfort the rejected. I will bring them to a deceptive state of peace, quiet, ease, calm, and contentment, to soothe their conscience by the works of their own hands. They will become their own god. Not to reject God's existence, but to question God's theology. Not to learn from him, but to form opinions with doubt and distrust in their minds. To create logic and speculation with reasoning. To resist in any way possible, by conflict or hidden deception, by carefully formed words of peace and unity in smooth persuasion to the unlearned . . . without them even noticing that it's been me all along."

Eve came to the tree of knowledge, even though there were many other trees all around. She remembered what Adam said, yet she saw *this* tree. As she drew near, this conflict was going to be the end of man's dominion over the earth. Satan knew it, though Eve and Adam had no clue of what was going to happen next.

Now the serpent was more subtle (cunning) than any beast of the field which the Lord God had made. And he said unto the woman, "Yea, hath God said, 'Ye shall not eat of every tree of the garden'?" And the woman said unto the serpent, "We may eat of the fruit of the trees of the garden: But of the fruit of the tree which is in the midst of the garden, God hath said, 'Ye shall not eat of it, neither shall ye touch it, lest ye die.'" And the serpent said unto the woman, "Ye shall not surely die." (Gen. 3:1–4)

For God doth know that in the day ye eat thereof, then your eyes shall be opened, and ye shall be as gods, knowing good and evil. And when the woman saw that the tree was good for food, and that it was pleasant to the eyes, and a tree to be desired to make one wise, she took of the fruit thereof, and did eat, and gave also unto her husband with her; and he did eat. And the eyes of them both were opened, and they knew that they were naked; and they sewed fig leaves together, and made themselves aprons. (Gen. 3:5–7)

The curse came upon the earth by death, sickness, and all the wickedness that came into the mind of humanity was now available for him to deliver to his victims.

Yet, even Satan had his limitations concerning what he could accomplish with man or beasts. If man agreed and walked with God's wisdom and knowledge, man would be protected. If he disagreed and rebelled, man would automatically bring upon himself the curse.

Man was accountable and responsible for his actions. Satan could only suggest and inspire through men's thoughts to accept what he used to tempt them with suggestions, and for demons to enter into men's bodies to fulfill their lustful nature.

This was the downfall of Eve and Adam. The human race fell. Yet God was always a step ahead. He knew that man would fall, and he understood that man was weak. Man could never save himself. He could never redeem himself in any form.

That is why God had a plan.

John, the Apostle of Jesus, wrote these words: "And all that dwell upon the earth shall worship him, whose names are not written in the book of life of the Lamb slain from the foundation of the world." (Rev. 13:8)

(Revelation speaks about the Great Tribulation, when the beast, the false prophet, and the image are worshiped. Those who worship them do not have their names written in the Lamb's book of life.)

The only reason that a lamb would be slain, was so that God clothed Adam and Eve with animal skins after a lamb was killed. That was a type, or an example, of Jesus the Christ, yet to come. For he would suffer for our sins.

"Unto Adam also and to his wife did the Lord God make coats of skins, and clothed them." (Gen. 3:21)

God would use these skins for clothing (Prov. 27:26).

Satan's next target would be Adam's son Cain, the firstborn.

Adam taught what he heard from God, as any father would. It doesn't speak of this in scripture, yet we know that the Bible speaks of raising our children in the Lord. Would not any good father do so? To speak of the amazing things God did and of his wonders?

We are going to read together from Deuteronomy chapter six.

I feel this is very important because many problems could have been resolved in children's lives as they grew older. If children would respect their parents, take heed, and obey them, they would have less problems.

"Honour thy father and thy mother: that thy days may be long upon the land which the Lord thy God giveth thee." (Exod. 20:12)

It would help if the parents studied from the Lord to be wise with the knowledge that they receive from the scriptures and to handle the scriptures properly.

We read from Deuteronomy chapter 6:

> Now these are the commandments, the statutes, and the judgments, which the Lord your God commanded to teach you, that ye might do them in the land whither ye go to possess it: That thou mightest fear the Lord thy God, to keep all his statutes and his commandments, which I command thee, thou, and thy son, and thy son's son, all the days of thy life; and that thy days may be prolonged. Hear therefore, O Israel, and observe to do it; that it may be well with thee, and that ye may increase mightily, as the Lord God of thy fathers hath promised thee, in the land that floweth with milk and honey. Hear, O Israel: The Lord our God is one Lord: And thou shalt love the Lord thy God with all thine heart, and with all thy soul, and with all thy might. And these words, which I command thee this day, shall be in thine heart: And thou shalt teach them diligently unto thy children, and shalt talk of them when thou sittest in thine house, and when thou walkest by the way, and when thou liest down, and when thou risest up. (Deut. 6:1–7)

Elsewhere, Deuteronomy chapter 4 says this:

> Now therefore hearken, O Israel, unto the statutes and unto the judgments, which I teach you, for to do them, that ye may live, and go in and possess the land which the Lord God of your fathers giveth you. Ye shall not add unto the word which I command you, neither shall ye diminish ought from it, that ye may keep the commandments of the Lord

your God which I command you. Your eyes have seen what the Lord did because of Baalpeor: for all the men that followed Baalpeor, the Lord thy God hath destroyed them from among you. But ye that did cleave unto the Lord your God are alive every one of you this day. Behold, I have taught you statutes and judgments, even as the Lord my God commanded me, that ye should do so in the land whither ye go to possess it. Keep therefore and do them; for this is your wisdom and your understanding in the sight of the nations, which shall hear all these statutes, and say, Surely this great nation is a wise and understanding people. For what nation is there so great, who hath God so nigh unto them, as the Lord our God is in all things that we call upon him for? And what nation is there so great, that hath statutes and judgments so righteous as all this law, which I set before you this day? Only take heed to thyself, and keep thy soul diligently, lest thou forget the things which thine eyes have seen, and lest they depart from thy heart all the days of thy life: but teach them thy sons, and thy sons' sons; Specially the day that thou stoodest before the Lord thy God in Horeb, when the Lord said unto me, Gather me the people together, and I will make them hear my words, that they may learn to fear me all the days that they shall live upon the earth, and that they may teach their children. (Deut. 4:1–10)

I cover the story about Cain and Abel in my first book, *Beyond Paradise: The Story of Our Ultimate Redemption.*

You can read it yourself. It reveals that Cain's offering was by works from the ground, and Abel's offering was an animal sacrifice by blood.

The reason why I speak of Cain is because we are going to learn that he was bitter and rebelled against the Lord, and by his influence his rebellion spread, his hidden anger and hate influenced his children and descendants.

Satan would spread this fear, anger, and hate throughout generations. Each of Cain's descendants had a choice to either serve the Lord's way, or their own way; to come to God's peace and understanding, or to go their own way.

We will see what it accomplished and how it relates to our culture and communities of today.

Cain's Children
and Civilizations

—ɯ—

The earth was experiencing the results of the curse by death, disease, and decay. Even though the earth was beautiful in many ways, man was corrupting the earth by the desires of his heart.

Generation after generation, it seemed that the world was changing; animals and people would become more violent and wicked than what they were before. Man seemed to come up with anything he could think of that would push the limit.

Like a child having no parents and striving to test the imagination of what was in its heart with reasoning and unrestrained thoughts. Many things were invented, and many buildings and temples (to other gods) were erected by the hands of men.

The elites would lift up their hearts in pride as they observed the skies, stars, sun, and moon. They developed secret teachings among themselves, and admitted those among them into their group, if they met their requirements for admission. They would take what God said and change it to fit their own interpretation.

THE OLD WORLD

The world before the flood was beautiful even though it was cursed after the fall of man, as God said.

At the creation of the earth, the land was gathered together into one place, which shows us it was one continent:

"And God said, 'Let the waters under the heaven be gathered together unto one place, and let the dry land appear:' and it was so. And God called the dry land Earth; and the gathering together of the waters called the Seas: and God saw that it was good." (Gen. 1:9–10)

In geology and earth sciences, this is what is found:

Pangaea or Pangea (/pæn'dʒi:ə/) was a super continent that existed during the late Paleozoic and
early Mesozoic eras. It assembled from earlier continental units approximately 335 million years ago,
and it began to break apart about 175 million years
ago. In contrast to the present earth and its distribution of continental mass, much of Pangaea was in
the southern hemisphere and surrounded by a super
ocean, Panthalassa. Pangaea was the most recent
super-continent to have existed and the first to be
reconstructed by geologists.

Many authors have written about this subject, concerning the creation of the earth. I'm sure you can research
it further, but Wikipedia does a good enough job.

There are good Christian creationist books that cover
this in more detail, and secular earth science books that
you can study.

As a believer in biblical studies, I don't agree with the
earth being that old.

The Bible reveals to us we have a young earth. Some
say under 10,000 years old, while others say around 6,000
years old. The world scoffs at such assumptions from their

viewpoint. Many do not receive the Resurrection of Christ, so we know where they stand.

My point was that the land was one continent. Genesis gives more clues about a divided earth after the flood.

"And unto Eber were born two sons: the name of one was Peleg; for in his days was the earth divided; and his brother's name was Joktan." (Gen. 10:25)

"Divided", from the Hebrew word *palag*, means to divide, to split.

God caused the earth to break up under the seas, which released untold amounts of water, while the water above the firmament came down as heavy rain. This caused large land masses to separate and spread apart.

Continental drift still happens today, but its name has been changed to plate tectonics.

"The idea of continental drift has been subsumed by the theory of plate tectonics which explains that the continents move by riding on plates of the Earth's crust" (Wikipedia).

Continuing:

> And it came to pass after seven days, that the waters of the flood were upon the earth. In the six hundredth year of Noah's life, in the second month, the seventeenth day of the month, the same day were all the fountains of the great deep broken up, and the windows of heaven were opened. And the rain was upon the earth forty days and forty nights. (Gen. 7:10–12)

After the flood, Noah and his family were on a completely different earth once the waters had receded. The world had changed and would continue to change.

YOU SHALL BE AS GODS

The people were of one language, one religion, or acceptance of other gods. We understand this by later texts that disclose this information.

"And the whole earth was of one language, and of one speech (*dabar*: business, occupation, acts, matter, case, something, manner (by extension))." (Gen. 11:1)

Those who sought after Adam's God did not worship themselves, the works of their own hands, or seducing spirits. It's interesting that this word "speech" (*dabar* in Hebrew) also means business, occupation, acts, matter, etc.

Could this be showing us that the world was an *economic order* as one people?

Does it reveal which gods they worshiped before the flood?

Yes, the same god that tempted Eve, saying, "You shall be as gods, knowing good and evil."

They also made themselves to be as gods, to be honored and worshiped because of their intelligence and the crafts they created.

Could this scripture reveal what was occurring before the flood according to what is written?

For the invisible things of him from the creation of the world are clearly seen, being understood by the things that are made, even his eternal power and Godhead; so that they are without excuse: Because that, when they knew God, they glorified him not as God, neither were thankful; but became vain in their imaginations, and their foolish heart was darkened. Professing themselves to be wise, they became fools, and changed the glory of the uncorruptible God into an image made like to corruptible man, and to birds, and fourfooted beasts, and creeping things. Wherefore God also gave them up to uncleanness through the lusts of their own hearts, to dishonour their own bodies between themselves: Who changed the truth of God into a lie, and worshipped and served the creature more than the Creator, who is blessed for ever. Amen. For this cause God gave them up unto vile affections: for even their women did change the natural use into that which is against nature: And likewise also the men, leaving the natural use of the woman, burned in their lust one toward another; men with men working that which is unseemly, and receiving in themselves that recompence of their error which was meet. And even as they did not like to retain God in their knowledge, God gave them over to a reprobate mind, to do those things which are not convenient; Being filled with all unrighteousness, fornication, wickedness, covetousness, maliciousness; full of envy, murder, debate, deceit, malignity; whisperers, backbiters, haters of God, despiteful, proud, boasters, inventors of evil things, disobedient to parents, without understanding, covenantbreakers, without natural affection, implacable, unmerciful: Who knowing the judgment of God, that they which commit such things are worthy of death, not only do the same, but have pleasure in them that do them. (Rom. 1:20–32)

This also looks very familiar, doesn't it? Yes. This type of culture and behavior spread before and after the flood of Noah, even to our civilization of today.

Paul spoke of something like it in the book of Timothy:

This know also, that in the last days perilous times shall come. For men shall be lovers of their own selves, covetous, boasters, proud, blasphemers, disobedient to parents, unthankful, unholy, without natural affection, trucebreakers, false accusers, incontinent, fierce, despisers of those that are good, traitors, heady, highminded, lovers of pleasures more than lovers of God; having a form of godliness, but denying the power thereof: from such turn away. (2 Tim. 3:1–5)

They had help also. Satan influenced them, and they went along with it.

Paul wrote of this to uncover pride, and not to lift up people as on a pedestal:

And these things, brethren, I have in a figure transferred to myself and to Apollos for your sakes; that ye might learn in us not to think of men above that which is written, that no one of you be puffed up (to inflate, blow up, to cause to swell up, pride) for one against another. For who maketh thee to differ from another? and what hast thou that thou didst not receive? now if thou didst receive it, why dost thou glory, as if thou hadst not received it? (1 Cor. 4:6–7)

God resists the proud. We all have received knowledge from someone or something.

"Likewise, ye younger, submit yourselves unto the elder. Yea, all of you be subject one to another, and be clothed with humility: for God resisteth the proud, and giveth grace to the humble. Humble yourselves therefore under the mighty hand of God, that he may exalt you in due time." (1 Pet. 5:5–6)

During those days, most people did not seek after God, yet we know that some people would hear and submit to his truth. They also followed their own rebellious ideas, which brought their death.

Notice what Peter tells us about those who were disobedient at times:

For Christ also hath once suffered for sins, the just for the unjust, that he might bring us to God, being put to death in the flesh, but quickened by the Spirit: By which also he went and preached unto the spirits in prison; Which sometime were disobedient, (unpersuaded) when once the longsuffering of God waited in the days of Noah, while the ark was a preparing, wherein few, that is, eight souls were saved by water. (1 Pet. 3:18–20)

A few points to think about: these spirits (humans who died) were sometimes disobedient or unpersuaded. That shows me that at times they were obedient. These spirits are those who died in Noah's time that trusted in God's plan of salvation by the blood, yet died in the flood.

"Unpersuaded", from the Greek word *apeitheō*, means to disbelieve (willfully and perversely—not believe, disobedient, obey not, unbelieving).

Plus, these spirits were in paradise (middle upper part of Sheol in the middle of the earth) waiting for Jesus. See Luke 16:22–31.

These people trusted in God's plan of salvation by the animal sacrifices, which were a type of Christ's suffering. My first book, *Beyond Paradise: The Story of Our Ultimate Redemption*, covers in detail about upper paradise and the great gulf that separates the lowest Sheol for the wicked and cursed (Luke 16:19–31).

In 1 Peter 3:20, it says, "They were saved by water." The word "saved" in Greek, *diasōzō*, means safety, ease, to preserve through danger, to bring safely through, to save out of danger, rescue (Acts 28:4, 27:44).

Noah and his family were saved by being aboard the Ark, which Noah prepared. They were saved from the coming judgment, which was a flood by water.

Let's continue:

The like figure whereunto even baptism doth also now save us (not the putting away of the filth of the flesh, but the answer of a good conscience toward God,) by the resurrection of Jesus Christ: Who is gone into heaven, and is on the right hand of God; angels and authorities and powers being made subject unto him. (1 Pet. 3:21–22)

ADAM'S FIRSTBORN

When we think about our children, we are eager for them to have a better life, to be successful, protected, and to be good examples toward others morally, and to be responsible for their actions, plus to come to a relationship with Christ, above all things.

We tend to think of the advantages they will have in their youth and strength to encourage their peers, to be caring and loving with honor and respect.

At times, we envision their life for the future and their unfulfilled dreams, waiting to be explored. Because of our love, prayers and desires indwell our minds, waiting for them to blossom maturely as we watch them develop.

When Adam found out that his son Abel was dead, it made him sick within himself. He couldn't believe it. Yet, he watched Cain have a change of character when he presented the fruits of the ground, and they were rejected by God.

Even though God was displeased with Cain, God told him, "If you do well, won't you be accepted?" God wanted the animal sacrifice, as Abel had offered, not the works of Cain's hands. It must be by blood, because it was a shadow of Jesus Christ's suffering to come.

We do not know how many times Adam tried to console Cain, and have him repent (change the mind) to seek after God's way.

They didn't know that the blood sacrifices would be an example of what God prepared for the future that Yahweh's only son Jesus would suffer according to the scriptures (Luke 24:26–27, 44–48; 1 Cor. 15:3; Ps. 69:9, 22:18; Isa. 50:6, 53:3–7).

Cain didn't go for that type of offering; plus it appears he didn't teach it to his children either.

As time went on, Cain's descendants sought something else: to exalt self by their works.

The world can influence us in many ways: the change of cultures, opinions by those in authority, media propaganda, and government that oversees our will and beliefs.

Popular consensus can make one an outcast, to be scorned and ridiculed, not to conform to what others believe.

We are about to read how this knowledge of invention and self-worth was going to be revealed.

We can see this by their testimony:

> And Cain went out from the presence of the Lord, and dwelt in the land of Nod, on the east of Eden. And Cain knew his wife; and she conceived, and bare Enoch: and he builded a city, and called the name of the city, after the name of his son, Enoch. And unto Enoch was born Irad: and Irad begat Mehujael: and Mehujael begat Methusael: and Methusael begat Lamech. (Gen. 4:16–18)

We ask ourselves, "Where did Cain's wife come from?" After Abel was killed, and after Cain left them, Adam and Eve had more children. In the process of time, their descendants had more children who spread across the world:

> And Adam knew his wife again; and she bare a son, and called his name Seth: For God, said she, hath appointed me another seed instead of Abel, whom Cain slew. And to Seth, to him also there was born a son; and he called his name Enos: then began men to call upon the name of the Lord. (Gen. 4:25–26)

Returning now to Genesis 4:17: "And Cain knew his wife; and she conceived, and bare Enoch: and he builded a city, and called the name of the city, after the name of his son, Enoch."

This could easily be passed over, as we read it, but if we look at this more closely, there are some very interesting points to think about.

THE CITY

Using the Young's Analytical Concordance to the Bible, let's look up the name of Enoch in Hebrew.

E-noch, He,-Noch, Tuition, teacher. Eldest of Cain. We must understand there were two Enoch's in the Bible. One was a son of Cain, and the other "Enoch", who was written about later, was the son of Jared.

What is interesting is that after Enoch was born, Cain built a city and named the city after his Son. Scripture gives no indication that Cain or his sons sought after the Lord.

There was another god (object of worship) of this world who would influence these men (2Cor 4:4). They would worship the works of their own hands just as their father before them had done.

When we study this word "tuition", we will receive an understanding of how this relates to Genesis 4:17. After all, "tuition" was the name that Cain gave to his son Enoch.

We probably have some idea what "tuition" means, but let's see what the dictionary has to offer.

From Wikipedia, the free encyclopedia:

Tuition payments, usually known as tuition in American English and as tuition fees in Commonwealth English are fees charged by education institutions for instruction or other services. Besides public spending (by governments and other public bodies), private spending via tuition payments are the largest revenue sources for education institutions in some countries. In most countries, especially countries in Scandinavia and Continental Europe, there are no or only nominal tuition fees for all forms of education, including university and other higher education.

Cain used his son's name as an example to *charge for higher learning*? Did I get that right? He named that city "Enoch": *Tuition*.

That's very interesting. Remember how hard Cain's heart was toward God's way of salvation (the blood offering), and he was *into the works of his own hands?*

Cain had killed his brother Abel because he didn't agree with him or his father's ways, which were God's ways.

Cain was becoming what we know of as a liberal. Why do I say that?

This is what it means in one dictionary: "Open to new behavior or opinions and willing to discard or change traditional values." There are many other dictionaries that give the same definition.

Just thinking about Cain, this was his character. He was resisting authority, God's commands, and God. He wanted to change things according to what he thought was right. He wanted his own freedom. Cain was in grave error.

Keep that in mind as we continue.

The word "teach" means to provide knowledge, to school, indoctrination, drill, to accustom to some action or attitude, method of passing on information or skill so that others may learn. This is from my Webster Dictionary; it's not online.

We are going to see a pattern here.

One man's rebellion would grow, as Satan would assist him. Remember also, this was generations before the flood of Noah.

Next, study this word: "city." This is the first time the word "city" is found in the Bible. (The first five books of the law are the Torah, and this includes the book of Genesis, written by Moses.)

A city is "an enclosed place where people gather together," according to Britannica.com

This says a city is a relatively permanent and highly organized center of population, of greater size or importance than a town or village. The name "city" is given to certain urban communities by virtue of some legal or conventional distinction that can vary between regions or nations. In most cases, however, the concept of city refers to a particular type of community, the urban community, and its culture, known as "urbanism."

We see it is a town or community of people who work, play, and exercise civil duties of government, and religious influence can also be present.

We will explore this more deeply with the foreknowledge that Cain and his sons did not seek after God—at least scripture doesn't show they walked with God.

MAN AND WIFE

Who would have imagined that this topic would be a subject of conversation and speculation? That it would become a talking point for debate and discussion? Yet, here we are, and humans feel they know what is best, in their own arrogance.

Starting with Genesis: "And Lamech took unto him two wives: the name of the one was Adah, and the name of the other Zillah" (Gen. 4:19).

(First mistake: God commanded man to have one wife (Gen. 2:24). It would be a curse to both men and kings by having more than one wife, because their hearts would draw them further away from God's laws. Many kings of the Bible had more than one wife. God did not approve of this since He knew the problems it would create, yet man has a free will.)

"And the Lord God said, 'It is not good that the man should be alone; I will make him a help meet for him.'" (Gen. 2:18)

God blessed Adam with a companion, Eve, a wife who made him complete.

The two beings became one flesh. *A symbol of marriage.*

It was never the intention of God for man to be *alone without a woman.*

It was not God's will for man to stay alone, quench the desire for intimacy and companionship of two being one-minded in love. God did not create anything unnatural, *that didn't procreate.*

This is not hate speech, but is fulfillment. *Marriage means to procreate.* Yet sinful humans have changed the definition of marriage over the years.

Marriage is what God wanted and ordained for thousands of years:

> And the rib, which the Lord God had taken from man, made he a woman, and brought her unto the man. And Adam said, "This is now bone of my bones, and flesh of my flesh: she shall be called Woman, because she was taken out of Man. Therefore shall a man leave his father and his mother, and shall cleave (joined to) unto his wife (Greek: woman, wife, female): and they shall be one flesh." And they were both naked, the man and his wife, and were not ashamed. (Gen. 2:22–25)

The Apostle Paul tells us:

> For this cause shall a man leave his father and mother, and shall be joined unto his wife, and they two shall be one flesh. This is a great mystery: but I speak

concerning Christ and the church. Nevertheless let every one of you in particular so love his wife even as himself; and the wife see that she reverence her husband. (Eph. 5:31–33)

Please read the entire chapter. It also reveals that Christ Jesus is the example as the bridegroom, and his church as the bride, "wife", which reveals one husband (male) and one wife (female).

We can either agree with God, or disagree, to our loss. Continuing in Genesis chapter 4:

And Adah bare Jabal: he was the father of such as dwell in tents, and of such as have cattle.

(So we see one who dwells in tents, and was a cattleman. This describes his business.) And his brother's name was Jubal: he was the father of all such as handle the harp and organ.

(Now we have Jubal, who was instructed in one of the liberal arts: music. Jubal = "stream", the son of Lamech by Adah and the inventor of musical instruments.)

And Zillah, she also bare Tubalcain, an instructer of every artificer in brass and iron: and the sister of Tubalcain was Naamah. (Gen. 4:20–22)

When we think of brass and iron, what do we think they were used for? Looking into these metals from the understanding we have today, we will also search how they were used in history. We have no actual records from the time before the flood of Noah, but only the information available from ancient Egyptian tombs, Babylon, Greek, and Roman historical scrolls, books, art, murals on pillars, walls, and floors from these civilizations and from prehistorical kingdoms that were in existence before the flood.

There is not much prehistoric history to investigate because cities fell into ruin and were lost in the sea. Deserts and forests overtook them, and the environment erased them in time. If anything had been written down, it would have been long gone through decay, unless recorded in stone or metal.

There is information we have of fallen cities and lost kingdoms that stir the imagination.

There are a few ideas to think about, some of which are based upon mythology, while others are based upon archaeological evidence.

KINGDOMS BEFORE THE FLOOD?

Atlantis (Ancient Greek: Ἀτλαντὶς νῆσος, "island of Atlas") is a fictional island mentioned in an allegory on the hubris of nations in Plato's works *Timaeus* and *Critias*, where it represents an antagonist naval power that besieges "ancient Athens", the pseudo-historic embodiment of Plato's ideal state in *The Republic*. In this story, Athens repels the Atlantean attack (where Atlantis is a nation unlike any other nation of the known world supposedly giving testament to the superiority of Plato's concept of a state. The story concludes with Atlantis falling out of favor with the deities and submerging into the Atlantic Ocean.

Despite its minor importance in Plato's work, the Atlantis story has had a considerable impact on literature. The allegorical aspect of Atlantis was written about in utopian works of several Renaissance writers, such as Francis Bacon's *New Atlantis* and Thomas Moore's *Utopia*. On the other hand, nineteenth century amateur scholars misinterpreted Plato's narrative as historical tradition, most notably in Ignatius L. Donnelly's *Atlantis: The Antediluvian World*. Plato's vague indications of the time of the events—more than 9,000 years before his time—and the alleged location of Atlantis—beyond the Pillars of Hercules—has led to much pseudoscientific speculation. As a consequence, Atlantis has become a byword for any and all supposed advanced, prehistoric, lost civilizations and continues to inspire contemporary fiction, from comic books to films (Wikipedia).

GÖBEKLI TEPE LOCATION: TURKEY.

This is very interesting.

It's one of the most mysterious structures ever discovered, and it inspires the imagination. Some people say the structure was built in 10,000 BC, which is based upon speculation, and it is located in today's southern Turkey. It's a series of nested, circular walls and steles, or monoliths, carved evocatively with animals. The place probably served as a temple for nomadic tribes in the area.

It was not a permanent residence, though it's possible a few priests lived there year-round. It is the first permanent human-built structure ever found, and probably represented the pinnacle of the local Mesopotamian civilization of its era. (The Bible does show the advancement of technology, during the days of Cain's descendants.)

BOSNIAN PYRAMID: OLDEST IN WORLD (25,000 YEARS OLD)

Two Italian archaeologists, Dr. Ricardo Brett and Niccolo Bisconti, found a piece of organic material on the pyramid in 2017. They were able to carbon date the material, and with it, the pyramid itself. This carbon dating places the pyramid 20,000 years before the Sumerian and Babylonian civilizations, believed to be some of the earliest in the world.

When the Bosnian Pyramid was first discovered in 2005, researchers could only measure the age of the topsoil covering the pyramid, which is about 12,000 years old.

SEA OF GALILEE, ISRAEL: 9,500 YEARS OLD

At the bottom of Israel's Lake Kinneret, also known as the Sea of Galilee, is a massive, enigmatic structure that could be more than 9,500 years old.

BIMINI ROAD: 12,000 YEARS OLD

Two camps of scientists have faced off on the issue of the underwater structure known as Bimini Road off the coast of the Bahamas since it was first discovered in 1968.

One camp says it is a 12,000–19,000-year-old man-made structure, flouting the conventional understanding that advanced civilizations only emerged 5,000 years ago. Some accept this, and others do not. This information can be found through a little research.

Yet, we know from the Bible that there were structures before the flood of Noah that Cain's sons built. The children of those times appear to be worshipping the works of their own hands and imaginations and reasoning without restraint.

Next, we will cover brass since that is mentioned in Genesis. The Bible tells us brass and iron existed much earlier than we have been taught according to history. Remember, it was before the flood of Noah. We will see what we can discover.

BRASS: ITS USAGE ACCORDING TO HISTORY

According to Cembrass, a company that has a production and sale of brass. They offer this information.

About 1400 BC, brass, which is an alloy of copper and zinc, was discovered and has an excellent property of great malleability in cold and in heat. It is also resistant to corrosion and wear.

Brass was used for vessels, dress armor, and jewelry by different kingdoms in that age. It was used also for coin, basins, lamps, bowls, jugs, and numerous other household items, and was used for engraved brass plates for depicting the deceased.

IRON: ITS USAGE AND ITS BEGINNINGS ACCORDING TO HISTORY

Iron is a chemical element with symbol Fe (from Latin: *ferrum*) and atomic number 26. It is a metal in the first transition series. It is, by mass, the most common element on Earth, forming much of Earth's outer and inner cores. It is the fourth most common element in the earth's crust.

Most iron is used to make steel—an alloy of iron and carbon— which in turn is used in manufacturing and civil engineering; for instance, to make reinforced concrete. Stainless steel, which contains at least ten percent chromium, is highly resistant to corrosion.

As we study, we can see the importance of iron in the development of ancient warfare.

According to sword making (Wikipedia):

Early swords were made of copper, which bends easily. Bronze swords were stronger; by varying the amount of tin in the alloy, a smith could make various parts of the sword harder or tougher to suit the demands of combat service. The Roman gladius was an early example of swords forged from blooms of steel.

Iron's importance rested in the fact that unlike bronze, which required the use of relatively rare tin to manufacture, iron was commonly and widely available almost everywhere.

Is it possible for these metals to have been used *before the flood of Noah*, though historical books tell us differently.

We did read in Genesis 4:22: "And Zillah, she also bare Tubalcain, an instructor of every artificer in brass and iron." *This is prehistory,* according to all the books you ever read about when brass and iron were used by civilizations. Yet these men before the flood had this knowledge.

The question is, "Who is this Tubalcain?"

I believe we will see what was in his heart and why he continued in rebellion as Cain had done: *to honor himself and take pride in the work of his hands.*

The Wikipedia says this: "Tubal-cain or Tubalcain (תּוּבַל קַיִן, Tūḇal Qayin) is a person mentioned in the Bible, in Genesis 4:22 as well as in the Hebrew Book of Jasher. He was a descendant of Cain, and the son of Lamech and Zillah. He was the brother of Naamah and half-brother of Jabal and Jubal and Noah (Gen. 5:30)."

Genesis 4:22 says that Tubalcain was the "forger of all instruments of bronze and iron" (ESV) or "an instructor of every artificer in brass and iron" (KJV). Although this may mean he was a metalsmith, a comparison with verses 20 and 21 suggests that he may have been the very first artificer in brass and iron.

T. C. Mitchell suggests that he "discovered the possibilities of cold forging native copper and meteoric iron." Tubalcain has even been described as the first chemist.

It's important to note that the inventions this man came up with weren't of his own doing. Since we know he did not seek after the Lord, did he receive influence from someone else? We do know in scriptures that humanity's sins would spread and become more evil.

"And Lamech said unto his wives, Adah and Zillah, 'Hear my voice; ye wives of Lamech, hearken unto my speech: for I have slain a man to my wounding, and a young man to my hurt'" (Gen. 4:23).

This gives us understanding that man was rejecting God's will. When God wanted man to have one wife, man chose two wives (Gen. 2:24–25).

God loved man and provided his way of salvation through the animal sacrifices. God wanted man to learn from his knowledge and understanding, not by the works of his own hands. It wasn't the advancements man achieved that were a threat to God. He knew who they were following, who influenced them, and the purpose behind it.

God allowed men to be driven by the *desires of their hearts*. Not to interfere, just as he had given Adam and Eve that choice.

Their own wickedness would be their downfall.

"And he shall bring upon them their own iniquity, and shall cut them off in their own wickedness; yea, the Lord our God shall cut them off" (Ps. 94:23).

Man rejected the ways of God and his instruction and allowed Satan to draw him away by his desires and the works of his own hands.

Yet there was coming a time that God would have enough of man's rebellion.

NOAH'S VISIBLE WARNING

—⚄—

One particular man was starting to build something. Trees were chopped down and were then used to create boards to form frames, planks, and ribs.

Initially, this man's neighbors did not take any notice, though eventually they asked him why he was building this structure. They wondered at first, *was this some type of storage for his goods, or maybe a home?*

When they asked, Noah just replied "God told" him. Noah could only say what God said.

With how much detail he spoke of, what he was doing is not known. Yet in the conversations he had with his neighbors, we can use our imagination.

The book of Genesis gives no scripture reference that Noah preached about a coming flood.

Yet his actions did show something different by the progress of his work. The scripture presented below might give us some idea about what he spoke: "And spared not the old world, but saved Noah the eighth person, a preacher of righteousness, bringing in the flood upon the world of the ungodly" (2 Pet. 2:5).

It is very interesting that Peter tells us that Noah was a preacher of righteousness. What did he preach? Maybe he learned from Adam and those that walked with God?

Additionally, it is very interesting that God spoke to the parents, and they would give names to their children in the Old Testament that might give some idea of what Noah preached.

What is the meaning of Noah's name? Noah's name in Hebrew, *Noach*, means "rest"; the tenth in descent from Adam.

Noah's name meaning "rest" is very interesting. We can only imagine what the people thought about him. This crazy man, building some type of large boat or structure . . . for what? Here was a man, creating beams and ribs, and setting them in place for years.

Noah worked on it every day, yet at a pace with ease, careful study, and diligence. He didn't let worldly pleasures or popularity affect him.

It seemed patience and skill was guiding him and the people of the city, towns, and villages would come to the area where Noah worked on his ark.

They mocked him, repeatedly laughing, and with gossip, saying, "What a fool, wasting his time." From the rich to the poor, from the high and mighty to the lowly esteemed, both young and old came to see this work.

They did not know it was a sign to them. It was a warning, but they placed little importance on it, or did not take heed. They lived their lives in the way they desired.

We do not know if the whole earth saw this ark, but I'm sure the news of this spread into all the world as they saw his progress over the years.

Noah was scorned, defamed, and was made a laughing stock before all.

Surely the close friends that Noah and his wife had were very concerned. They questioned, were offended, and eventually separated themselves from Noah's company.

Though their reputation might be ruined, Noah and his family did not worry about what others might say or think on the work he was doing.

Even though God spoke to Noah about this work, it was not every day, week, or year that he had this conversation with God, according to Scripture.

Neither do we know if it was an audible voice that Noah heard, or that small still voice through which God speaks to us (1 Kings 19:11–13).

Can we consider the pressure of doubt and reasoning that Satan would try to place on him?

Satan could have said these words to him: "Is there a flood coming? What if I'm wrong? Suppose I don't finish it before God starts his destruction? How will my wife handle it…and my children? Will the people become angry with me, for one reason or another? Am I in my right mind? Am I prideful man?"

Surely Satan and his devils tried anything and everything they could think of, yet Noah was diligent and steadfast. He submitted his will and his heart to God.

Since Noah was human, it was hard at times with this pressure, what he faced every day, I'm sure of it.

We all can agree, because we all face temptations and trials that come into our lives. Yet, Noah continued trusting God and working by faith:

> By faith (steadfastness) Noah, being warned of God of things not seen as yet, moved with fear (eulabeomai–to act cautiously, to reverence, to stand in awe of), prepared an ark to the saving of his house; by the which he condemned the world, and became heir of the righteousness which is by faith. (Heb. 11:7)

Noah started this project when his sons were born, and the ark was finished one hundred years later.

Noah was five hundred years old when he started it. "And Noah was five hundred years old: and Noah begat Shem, Ham, and Japheth" (Gen. 5:32).

Noah was six hundred years old when the flood came. "In the six hundredth year of Noah's life, in the second month, the seventeenth day of the month, the same day were all the fountains of the great deep broken up, and the windows of heaven were opened" (Gen. 7:11).

Noah revealed his faith by doing the job that God commanded him; not focusing on anything else except what was for the future. By his obedience and God's help, he saved his family, himself, and allowed humanity to have another chance. If it was not for Noah, we wouldn't be here. Think on that.

THE JUDGMENT

The clouds started to gather over the world through an unseen force that became determined to cover the sun, and the air currents pushed atmospheric cells building massive thunderheads. Clouds heavy with warm air moved upward, and the water vapor condensed into storm systems. Then rain started to come down on the earth in the valleys, forests, mountains, and seashores—all over the world.

In seconds, the rain increased, with small rivers turning into massive streams, rushing into locations where there was no water before. Small floods were destroying all types of agriculture and developments. Both animals and people were washed away. Small villages vanished as the rush of water from above and below destroyed and wiped them out.

Homes, villages, and man's structures were being invaded, as a living force was taking vengeance without mercy, destroying without prejudice. Generations lost, from old age to youth.

On the seacoasts, the land started to sink, becoming massive quicksand pits in many areas as it swallowed thousands of people desperately trying to cling on to life. Loved ones, parents, and children were separated forever. A mix of heavy rain and soil under people's feet quickly became unstable.

Mountainous hills near the seacoasts were melting into the sea. Large landmasses were crumbling into the waters each minute. Tens of thousands of voices became silent.

Statues and buildings fell over with no effort.

The sea and the rain also mixed together, causing great landslides, covering untold hundreds of thousands of people in tombs pushed down to the sea bottom.

Large animals were killed as the flood was creating sinkholes and causing trees to fall and kill them or drown them. Forests were destroyed as the flood covered them like a blanket.

Massive walls of water would turn the valleys into instant lakes for a few minutes which would then disappear as the waters increased, overflowing onto other locations of higher ground.

The waters above the firmament came down at the same time as the rain from the clouds.

In Genesis 1:6–9, firmament (the Hebrew word *raqiya*) means extended surface (solid), expanse, firmament.

The earth below started to breakup on the sea bottom by volcanic activity, which added more water from these huge pockets within the earth.

This happened very quickly and at the same time. There was no safe place as the remaining small groups of people fought to keep alive on the highest mountains, which were now spotted hills on the sea. These hills were melting away as the rain continued to come down.

"In the six hundredth year of Noah's life, in the second month, the seventeenth day of the month, the same day were all the fountains of the great deep broken up, and the windows of heaven were opened" (Gen. 7:11).

At first, some people thought this was nothing to be concerned with as they looked out from inside their homes and from the locations of their cities, towns, villages, and fields. They remembered that for one hundred years, a man called Noah was building some type of structure. Then they became fearful as the waters became higher and threatening. They weren't laughing anymore. Terror was chasing them, and there was no escape.

The people of the earth were trying to find higher ground as their places of safety were destroyed, and the weight of rain destroyed the roofs of their homes. The earth below their feet started to breakup, as if being swallowed by a great creature. There was no time to grieve for loss because it was a time of desperation with unimaginable emotional stress for survival.

This revealed man's worst behavior toward one another. They no longer spoke with tenderness, care, and love, but now fought to reach higher ground, taking whatever supplies and weapons they could carry to protect themselves.

Death was slaying them in untold numbers. As large landmasses were melting into the seas, raging tidal waves were smashing and covering their civilization forever.

Small tops of high mountains still could be seen around the world, as the rain continued. Small groups of people were pushed into the sea as wind and water covered the last parts of land. In desperation, they were trying to stay above the surface, as the waves sent some of them into the depths below. Some looked into the faces of others as they struggled to tread water with the rain coming down and the oceans' violent anger against them. Others watched loved ones descending below as the last of their strength also was drained; even the strongest swimmers would fail.

The skies thundered and rain poured and offered no rescue, but certain destruction. Only one structure could be seen, guided by an unseen hand, as mountainous, gigantic waves tossed the ark back and forth on a world of water.

All life on the land was destroyed. Noah, his wife, and his three sons, and their wives were protected on the Ark, along with the animals, birds, and other creatures.

God's judgment came, and what God said came to pass. When God makes a promise, he keeps it.

It rained for forty days and forty nights, and all life on earth was destroyed (Gen. 7:1–6, 17).

The world will not truly fear God, *until they see him move*. Then it might be too late.

THE WORLD BEFORE THE FLOOD

—॥⋙—

From the beginning of the world, the earth was a very different place than what we have today. There were massive forests and plant life that were lush and beautiful. The air was clean and pleasurable to the sight and smell. God created an amazing greenhouse that kept the earth well-watered and alive. There were untold species of plants and fruits of which we might have never seen that became extinct because of the flood.

God prepared a mist from the heavens to water the earth. There was also a canopy of water above the firmament of the earth: "But there went up a mist from the earth, and watered the whole face of the ground" (Gen. 2:6).

God used this canopy of water to filter out radiation from the sun. Those who have studied the science of biblical creation understand the waters above the earth reduced the rays that would otherwise penetrate to the earth's surface.

Here is a short list, just to name a few: There are solar, gamma, ultraviolet, radio, and microwave rays. You can search in books to learn about them, but Wikipedia does a good job on this.

The canopy of water protected the earth and those on it. Large animals roamed the earth along with large insects, and large sea animals swam in the ocean. We can understand this from fossilized plants, insects, and animals.

There were all types of animals, including some that we would call dinosaurs. The taxon *Dinosauria* was formally named in 1841 by paleontologist Sir Richard Owen, who used it to refer to the "distinct tribe or sub-order of Saurian Reptiles" that were then being recognized in England and around the world. The term is derived from Ancient Greek δεινός (*deinos*), meaning "terrible, potent or fearfully great", and σαῦρος (*sauros*), meaning "lizard or reptile."

These beasts were in the seas and on the land, and were of different types and sizes.

I am not going to cover this topic because there are many excellent books on the subject of creation that cover dinosaurs.

Man's age was also amazing. His lifespan was hundreds of years. In fact, the oldest man recorded was Methuselah, who lived 969 years (Gen. 5:27).

It would seem these people would live forever. This gave them plenty of time for work, pleasure, and to have more children. Wouldn't you like to work for hundreds of years? Well, we won't go there. I can imagine what kind of answer you would have.

If anyone heard about these people's ages and the world they lived in a few thousand years after the flood, wouldn't it seem like a golden age? Would these people appear like gods in their eyes?

After a few hundred years, it would not mean anything to Noah's grandchildren because he would inform them what type of people they were like before the flood. After the flood, lifespans would decrease to the current normal age of seventy or eighty years, according to Psalm 90:10–12.

The time of these people before the flood, would be considered as an *age of enlightenment and vast knowledge*. The extent of their technology, civilization, and inventions had been lost. However, this is hinted in Genesis chapter

4. The descendants of Noah and his family would imagine that these people were gods because of their extensive lost knowledge and age. This gave birth to the idea of gods through legends and mythology in many cultures around the world.

In Genesis chapter 10, we are told: "These are the families of the sons of Noah, after their generations, in their nations: and by these were the nations divided in the earth after the flood" (Gen. 10:32).

The things that were experienced, seen, and known before the flood, would then be remembered by Noah's children and his children's children, as they spread their ideas across the world.

CHANGE OF THE WORLD

We can research for ourselves that many types of species are no longer with us because of extinction of these creatures, either by man or natural disasters.

We do know that the water cycle involves the processes of water evaporation, cloud formation, and precipitation. Did it rain before the flood of Noah? Some have debated this subject. However, it never flooded again as it did during the flood of Noah.

The seasons would change after the flood, especially since it appears that there were no seasons before the flood. There is nothing written on this until Genesis 8:20–22:

> And Noah builded an altar unto the Lord; and took of every clean beast, and of every clean fowl, and offered burnt offerings on the altar. And the Lord smelled a sweet savour; and the Lord said in his heart, I will not again curse the ground any more for man's sake; for the imagination of man's heart is evil from his youth; neither will I again smite any more every thing living, as I have done. While

the earth remaineth, seedtime and harvest, and cold and heat, and summer and winter, and day and night shall not cease.

This is the first time seasons are mentioned in the Bible. As we continue to read, we can see the world is changing with these seasons on the earth, but man's heart would be evil from his youth (Gen. 8:21). That hasn't changed and the evil would continue to increase.

Yet God would not destroy the world with a *flood ever again*, because he promised this:

"I do set my bow in the cloud, and it shall be for a token of a covenant between me and the earth" (Gen. 9:13).

And I will remember my covenant, which is between me and you and every living creature of all flesh; and the waters shall no more become a flood to destroy all flesh. And the bow shall be in the cloud; and I will look upon it, that I may remember the everlasting covenant between God and every living creature of all flesh that is upon the earth. And God said unto Noah, "This is the token of the covenant, which I have established between me and all flesh that is upon the earth." (Gen. 9:15–17)

God made this promise, but he also made another promise that he would *destroy the world with fire*. We will talk about that later.

The water above the firmament had never come down previously as it did during Noah's Flood. We know that it was a type of greenhouse on the earth, since the Bible says there was a canopy of water above the firmament from its creation.

Wouldn't this cause a magnification effect? The sun, moon, planets, and stars could be clearly seen, and would appear larger. The stars would appear closer, as though hanging over the mountains. This would add wonderment and a curiosity to understand what God created.

SEEDS IN THE MIND

Satan would plant a seed in people's minds for them to learn about nature and to honor it, to create spiritualism, and to consider how nature, the stars, and planets might relate to humans. Satan would turn the beautiful things of God into objects of worship and mystery in their eyes.

The word "worship" refers to having some type of spiritual mystery and reverence.

Webster tells us this:

1. to honor or reverence as a divine being or supernatural power
2. to regard with great or extravagant respect, honor, or devotion.

Devotion focuses our time, desires, and income into those things at times.

The enlightened would study the sun and moon and measure them by observing their locations and the paths they would travel in the sky. The sun rising and setting, and the stars in the constellations would be given names through traditions, myths, and legends.

The cycles of the moon, sun, stars, and planets—and how they are related to nature, crops, government, and a type of spiritual understanding of philosophy—are an influence to man.

We can find references to these things in old temples and tombs of Egyptians, Babylonians, Greeks, Romans, Chinese, etc. as the *gods of the constellations*.

Collectively they are known as *the zodiac*, and as the *host of heaven* (in the Bible), something which God commanded men not to worship:

And God spake all these words, saying, "I am the Lord thy God, which have brought thee out of the land of Egypt, out of the house of bondage. Thou shalt have no other gods before me. Thou shalt not make unto thee any graven image, or any likeness of any thing that is in heaven above, or that is in the earth beneath, or that is in the water under the earth. Thou shalt not bow down thyself to them, nor serve them: for I the Lord thy God am a jealous God, visiting the iniquity of the fathers upon the children unto the third and fourth generation of them that hate me." (Exod. 20:1–5)

Here is an example of what was in the hearts of the priests:

And the king commanded Hilkiah the high priest, and the priests of the second order, and the keepers of the door, to bring forth out of the temple of the Lord all the vessels that were made for Baal, and for the grove, and for all the host of heaven: and he burned them without Jerusalem in the fields of Kidron, and carried the ashes of them unto Bethel. And he put down the idolatrous priests, whom the kings of Judah had ordained to burn incense in the high places in the cities of Judah, and in the places round about Jerusalem; them also that burned incense unto Baal, to the sun, and to the moon, and to the planets, and to all the host of heaven. (2 Kings 23:4–5)

"And they left all the commandments of the Lord their God, and made them molten images, even two calves, and made a grove, and worshipped all the host of heaven, and served Baal." (2 Kings 17:16)

God created the things of nature for man to enjoy and learn from, not to worship them above God. Again:

> And God spake all these words, saying, "I am the Lord thy God, which have brought thee out of the land of Egypt, out of the house of bondage. Thou shalt have no other gods before me. Thou shalt not make unto thee any graven image, or any likeness of any thing that is in heaven above, or that is in the earth beneath, or that is in the water under the earth. Thou shalt not bow down thyself to them, nor serve them: for I the Lord thy God am a jealous God, visiting the iniquity of the fathers upon the children unto the third and fourth generation of them that hate me." (Exod. 20:1–5)

"By the word of the Lord were the heavens made; and all the host of them by the breath of his mouth." (Ps. 33:6)

These civilizations did not worship the images they set up as if they were alive, per se, but rather, they represented contact with those gods or spirits and how they related to their personal life.

This is what God commanded Moses when he led the Israelites out of Egypt. Moses was raised under Pharaoh's daughter, experienced this, and knew of their gods. However, Moses was also taught by his natural mother about the God of Israel.

Moses taught the people later in the wilderness not to honor images, statues, or monuments dedicated to themselves and to their gods, which were made after the likeness of the heavens, humans, and the creatures on the earth. This is what God commanded Moses to do.

Recognition: The Friend of Pride

It appears that humans still would not accept the idea of not having other gods, which started after Eve and Adam's rebellion. We must remember that the word "god" in Hebrew means "an object of worship." There are hundreds of scriptures that refer to this subject.

We have seen in scripture that Satan tempted Eve and Adam with this desire to be "*as gods, knowing good and evil.*"

Cain and his descendants also faced this temptation. This idea of being objects of worship would spread for generations. Because of the honor of "self", man would fall deeper into sin, wanting recognition from the deeds and works of their own hands.

According to the dictionary, this word recognition means:

rec·og·ni·tion' rekəg' niSH(ə)n/

Noun. The action or process of recognizing or being recognized, in particular.

synonyms: identification, recollection, remembrance

identification of a thing or person from previous encounters or knowledge.

"she saw him pass by without a sign of recognition"

synonyms: identification, recollection, remembrance

"there was no sign of recognition on his face"

acknowledgment of something's existence, validity, or legality.

"the unions must receive proper recognition"

synonyms: acknowledgment, acceptance, admission; realization, awareness, consciousness, knowledge, appreciation; formal cognizance

"his recognition of his lack of experience"

official approval, certification, accreditation, endorsement, validation

"the sport has finally received the recognition it deserves"

This was the problem. Because man would invent something (so he claimed), he would lift himself up with pride in his accomplishments.

What is worse is a humble type of pride—to display a performance of humility, yet really a desire for attention, recognition, validation, and the praise of men.

Jesus did not seek after this, and as his people, should we? We should seek to please him, not ourselves. Are we trying to honor and glorify ourselves, or to give honor to him?

I try to follow after his example, because I know his way is best. At times, we all will slip and fall, but we can always go to him and acknowledge our faults.

When I read what he said, it's absolutely clear what God desires for us: not to be seduced by Satan with arrogance, pride, and self-importance, because he will take you on a journey that you may not like later if you're seeking to serve and trust Christ. With pride, *there is always a fall*, sooner or later.

The next chapter will prove to be very thought-provoking.

The world before the flood had amazing technology and advancements. We will never know while we are here on Earth what inventions they created. We can only speculate by the archaeological evidence and what sciences we have today.

Since the curse was on the earth, sin was spreading after the rebellion of Cain. This affected the whole world and the world will never be the same until God creates a New Heaven (atmosphere) and Earth. That is for the future.

One World System.

I am taking the time to cover this belief because this same worldview existed both before the flood and after, even though all the population was destroyed in the flood of Noah.

Noah and his family survived, had children, and their descendants eventually spread over the world. The world had one language as before the flood, which helped in business, commerce, and trade, and once again, technology increased.

Buildings were constructed and raised, just as man's ego did.

Today, in our modern times, we have heard about a "New World Order" or a "Global Economic Order." There are many views on this over the years from presidents, as well as from economists and religious leaders. Some views are radical, and some are less radical. Yet, the Bible does reveal that there is something legitimate about this statement. Read the scriptures below and see for yourself.

The world after the flood had one language. There was a one-world system:

> And the whole earth was of one language, and of one speech. And it came to pass, as they journeyed from the east, that they found a plain in the land of Shinar; and they dwelt there. And they said one to another, Go to, let us make brick, and burn them thoroughly. And they had brick for stone, and slime

had they for morter. And they said, "Go to, let us build us a city and a tower, whose top may reach unto heaven; and let us make us a name, lest we be scattered abroad upon the face of the whole earth." And the Lord came down to see the city and the tower, which the children of men builded. And the Lord said, "Behold, the people is one, and they have all one language; and this they begin to do: and now nothing will be restrained from them, which they have imagined to do. Go to, let us go down, and there confound their language, that they may not understand one another's speech." So the Lord scattered them abroad from thence upon the face of all the earth: and they left off to build the city. Therefore is the name of it called Babel; because the Lord did there confound the language of all the earth: and from thence did the Lord scatter them abroad upon the face of all the earth. (Gen. 11:1–9)

God changed their language, which was the same before the flood and after. "Language" (in Hebrew: *saphah*) in Genesis 11:1 means "lip, language, speech, shore, bank, brink, brim, side, edge, border, binding."

"Speech" (in Hebrew: *dabar*) means "speech, word, speaking, thing, business, occupation, acts, matter, case, something, manner (by extension)."

This shows us the world was one in many aspects. Yet those who stood for the Lord, as Noah did, I'm sure were riddled with ridicule.

By reading other scriptures, we can see a pattern of behavior from these people before and after the flood.

We can search for other scriptures to give us an idea of how they behaved. Here are a few, I think, we should consider:

Paul wrote this to the church in Rome, which was a mix of different people. Jews, Romans, Greeks, and Barbarians came to the saving knowledge of the Lord Jesus (Romans 1:5–8, 13–14).

Paul encouraged them and shared with them what God had called him to do. He then shared about the unrighteousness of man, and man's nature:

> For I am not ashamed of the gospel of Christ: for it is the power of God unto salvation to every one that believeth; to the Jew first, and also to the Greek. For therein is the righteousness of God revealed from faith to faith: as it is written, The just (justified) shall live by faith. For the wrath of God is revealed from heaven against all ungodliness and unrighteousness of men, who hold the truth in unrighteousness; because that which may be known of God is manifest in them; for God hath shewed it unto them. For the invisible things of him from the creation of the world are clearly seen, being understood by the things that are made, even his eternal power and Godhead; so that they are without excuse: Because that, when they knew God, they glorified him not as God, neither were thankful; but became vain in their imaginations, and their foolish heart was darkened. Professing themselves to be wise, they became fools, and changed the glory of the uncorruptible God into an image made like to corruptible man, and to birds, and fourfooted beasts, and creeping things. Wherefore God also gave them up to uncleanness through the lusts of their own hearts, to dishonour their own bodies between themselves: Who changed the truth of God into a lie, and worshipped and served the creature more than the Creator, who is blessed for ever. Amen. For this cause God gave them up unto vile affections: for even their women did change the natural use into that which is against nature: And likewise

also the men, leaving the natural use of the woman, burned in their lust one toward another; men with men working that which is unseemly, and receiving in themselves that recompence of their error which was meet. And even as they did not like to retain God in their knowledge, God gave them over to a reprobate mind, to do those things which are not convenient; being filled with all unrighteousness, fornication, wickedness, covetousness, maliciousness; full of envy, murder, debate, deceit, malignity; whisperers, backbiters, haters of God, despiteful, proud, boasters, inventors of evil things, disobedient to parents, without understanding, covenantbreakers, without natural affection, implacable, unmerciful: Who knowing the judgment of God, that they which commit such things are worthy of death, not only do the same, but have pleasure in them that do them. (Rom. 1:16–32)

There is so much information here, I would advise you to study it.

This type of human nature existed before the flood and after, and continues to this very day.

Was the example "of the Days of Noah" that Jesus spoke of, an example of the times coming (Matt. 24:37)?

Will the world come together?

Was the Babylonian city and tower a sign showing how the world would come together in the future? Would social, economic, cultural, and religious organizations be incorporated? It's something to think about.

Next, we are going to look at Genesis 6 to see how God saw men's hearts.

This should be very interesting because of how it will relate to the days of which Jesus spoke. Other men of God from the Bible also wrote about the last days.

THE GENERATION OF DESTRUCTION

—⁂—

There was wickedness on the earth. It filled every home, building, village, monument, and statue on the earth. The people went into corruption beyond imagination. In fact, their imaginations and thoughts were far worse than those of Cain.

Satan was overseeing their ignorance and rebellion to bring about what he desired: to provoke the God of Heaven to be disgusted by their deeds; to destroy humanity and to make a mockery of his creation.

This was Satan's plan all long. Speaking to Eve, saying, "You shall be as gods knowing good and evil."

Satan tempted men and women with knowledge and wisdom to become demigods as *giants in their own eyes*. To rule over those with less education in their sight. To promote the imaginations of their hearts without restraint. To ignore God's ways and what they heard from Adam and those that walked with God. Just as Satan lifted himself up with pride in heaven, they did likewise.

To justify their pride by preconceived revelation through some spiritualistic way of thinking. They did not fear the consequences.

They were in rebellion against God and the rebellion was spreading like a bush-fire.

The Bible speaks of these truths concerning this behavior in both the Old Testament and the New Testament.

Notice what Solomon says:

> Because sentence against an evil work is not executed speedily, therefore the heart of the sons of men is fully set in them to do evil. Though a sinner do evil an hundred times, and his days be prolonged, yet surely I know that it shall be well with them that fear God, which fear before him: But it shall not be well with the wicked, neither shall he prolong his days, which are as a shadow; because he feareth not before God. (Eccl. 8:11–13)

God is patient, loving, and giving. We have no idea how far God is able to be pushed.

Yet we ask, isn't he God? Doesn't he know all this will happen? Yes, he knows, but God does have his limits.

We can only understand God's character by what the prophets wrote down, and by what Jesus said and did, and additionally by what his disciples and servants taught through the Holy Ghost.

We can tell how people were influenced by what they heard and learned from God's written Word.

Adam and those who agreed with God did not have a whole lot of scripture verses to stand on back then. However, they did have their conscience to discern between good and evil after the fall. Yet, man seems to go in another direction by following the desires of the flesh and mind through *reasoning and logic*.

As we study and read God's Word, it will influence us toward better things.

God's Word shall guide us into all truth, and then good deeds will be seen.

GOOD FRUIT AND WORKS OF THE FLESH

Look at this example: Satan tempts a believer in the parable of the seed and sower. The seed is the written Word of God.

"He also that received seed among the thorns is he that heareth the word; and the care (distractions) of this world, and the deceitfulness of riches, choke the word, and he becometh unfruitful" (Matt. 13:22).

When we allow both the distractions and riches of the world to influence us, we become unfruitful. These things will distract us, from what the Lord truly desires in our lives, which is the fruit of the spirit:

> But the fruit of the Spirit is love, joy, peace, longsuffering, gentleness, goodness, faith, meekness, temperance: against such there is no law. And they that are Christ's have crucified the flesh with the affections and lusts (over desires). If we live in the Spirit, let us also walk in the Spirit. Let us not be desirous of vain glory, provoking one another, envying one another. (Gal. 5:22–26)

This fruit also is what we do for the Lord in our life, according to where he placed us for his work in the body of Christ. If we feel we need more peace, joy, and gentleness, we should seek what the Lord said through his servants in the Bible. We learn by reading about their examples, which builds our faith.

Our fruit can be corrupted by wrong desires, decisions, and objectives.

We can grow distracted by various temptations, which cause the fruit of our spirit to become tarnished.

Here is another scripture that will be useful: "And that which fell among thorns are they, which, when they have heard, go forth, and are choked with cares (distractions) and riches and pleasures of this life, and bring no fruit to perfection (completeness)" (Luke 8:14).

Study both these sections in Matthew 13 and Luke 8 on the seed and sower. From these scriptures alone, we can see how people behaved both before the flood and after.

CULTURE CHANGE

When God says "wickedness" in the scriptures, he means it. Its culture, government, worship, behavior in social interactions, and relationships between male and female, plus the pride of advancement through inventions and technology.

These next scriptures show the behavior of the flesh:

This I say then, "Walk in the Spirit, and ye shall not fulfil the lust of the flesh. For the flesh lusteth against the Spirit, and the Spirit against the flesh: and these are contrary the one to the other: so that ye cannot do the things that ye would. But if ye be led of the Spirit, ye are not under the law. Now the works of the flesh are manifest, which are these; adultery, fornication (the Greek word means illicit sexual intercourse (including adultery and incest; figuratively, idolatry:—fornication), uncleanness (in a moral sense: the impurity of lustful, luxurious, profligate living), lasciviousness (unbridled lust, excess, licentiousness, lasciviousness, outrageousness, shamelessness, insolence), idolatry (the worship of false gods, idolatry), witchcraft (the use or the administration of drugs, sorcery, magical arts, often found in connection with idolatry, and fostered by it), hatred (passion, angry, heat, anger forthwith boiling up and soon subsiding again), variance (contention, strife, wrangling), emulations (excitement of mind, ardour, fervour of spirit), wrath (passion, angry, heat, anger forthwith boiling up and soon subsiding again), strife, seditions (dissension, division), heresies (dissensions arising from diversity of opinions and aims), envyings, murders, drunkenness (intoxication), revellings (reveling, rioting) and such like: of the which I tell you before, as I have also told you in time past, that they which do such things shall not inherit the kingdom of God." (Gal. 5:16–21)

To be honest, at one time or another, we all have exhibited some or most of the characteristics from this list. As long we are in this body, we might repeat some things from this list since our body is earthly, and we must bring it into subjection to God's Word by the Holy Ghost.

Rebellion, envy, lust (over desire), hate, and strife, which are the most common to man, can influence us. Most will agree that we can give in to this behavior, which is unacceptable behavior.

It says in the Bible, "I have also told you in time past, that they which do such things shall not inherit the kingdom of God."

What was Paul saying? "If you behave with hate, envy, or strife, will that alone cause you not to inherit the kingdom of God"?

To begin with, of which kingdom are we speaking? The kingdom within, by his spirit (Luke 17:21)? Or of his coming kingdom, when Jesus rules as King of kings, and Lord of lords during his one-thousand-year reign on Earth?

If you read carefully in this chapter, Paul is talking about our behavior and the kingdom within us, by faith.

Jesus' physical kingdom will come later. If we allow wicked behavior to overcome us, we will not be able to inherit the fullness of the spirit because we are walking in the flesh. *If we are not saved, or born again,* any sin would bring judgment after we die *because we are already in a lost and condemned state.*

The apostle John writes:

> For God so loved the world, that he gave his only begotten Son, that whosoever believeth (rely and trust on) in him should not perish, but have everlasting life. For God sent not his Son into the world to condemn the world; but that the world through him might be saved. He that believeth on him is not condemned: but he that believeth not is condemned already, because he hath not believed in the name of the only begotten Son of God. (John 3:16–18)

Along with many other scriptures, this shows us that we are condemned already until we believe (rely and trust) in the name of the only begotten (only born) of God.

Read all of Galatians. Paul reveals in detail what Jesus did for us and how he brought us salvation. We need to believe that his blood saved us (1 John 1:7) and washed away our sins, and that God raised Jesus from the dead (Acts 2:24) to have eternal life (1 John 5:13–14). Then call on Jesus Christ (Romans 10:9–10) and you will be saved:

> That if thou shalt confess with thy mouth the Lord Jesus, and shalt believe in thine heart that God hath raised him from the dead, thou shalt be saved. For with the heart man believeth unto righteousness; and with the mouth confession is made unto salvation. For the scripture saith, "Whosoever believeth on him shall not be ashamed. For there is no difference between the Jew and the Greek: for the same Lord over all is rich unto all that call upon him. For

whosoever shall call upon the name of the Lord shall be saved." (Rom. 10:9–13)

CAN ANGELS PROCREATE?

As we read Genesis 6, we will see how the Lord described the wickedness of those times: "And it came to pass, when men began to multiply on the face of the earth, and daughters were born unto them, 'That the sons of God saw the daughters of men that they were fair; and they took them wives of all which they chose'" (Gen. 6:1–2).

Some organizations in the church and the mythologies of different cultures teach that these sons of God were angels that came down and had sex with the daughters of men.

Notice what Jesus had to say on this subject:

> The same day came to him the Sadducees, which say that there is no resurrection, and asked him, saying, "Master," Moses said, "If a man die, having no children, his brother shall marry his wife, and raise up seed unto his brother. Now there were with us seven brethren: and the first, when he had married a wife, deceased, and, having no issue, left his wife unto his brother: Likewise the second also, and the third, unto the seventh. And last of all the woman died also. Therefore in the resurrection whose wife shall she be of the seven? for they all had her." Jesus answered and said unto them, "Ye do err, not knowing the scriptures, nor the power of God. For in the resurrection they neither marry, nor are given in marriage, but are as the angels of God in heaven." (Matt. 22:23–30)

Jesus was explaining the Resurrection to them and that they would be as the *angels of heaven* that are neither *male nor female*. Angels neither have the parts needed to pro-create, nor blood, for that matter.

A spirit does not have flesh, bone, and blood as we do.

A spirit is known in the Bible as ministering spirit: "But to which of the angels said he at any time, Sit on my right hand, until I make thine enemies thy footstool? Are they not all ministering spirits, sent forth to minister for them who shall be heirs of salvation?" (Heb. 1:13–14)

> But they were terrified and affrighted, and supposed that they had seen a spirit. And he said unto them, "Why are ye troubled? and why do thoughts arise in your hearts?" And he said unto them, "Why are ye troubled? And why do thoughts arise in your hearts? Behold my hands and my feet, that it is I myself: handle me, and see; for a spirit hath not flesh and bones, as ye see me have." (Luke 24:37–39)

Angels come from heaven and have no flesh or blood:

"And as we have borne the image of the earthy, we shall also bear the image of the heavenly. Now this I say, brethren, that flesh and blood cannot inherit the kingdom of God; neither doth corruption inherit incorruption" (1 Cor. 15:49–50)

These scriptures give us an understanding that a spirit cannot marry, and that angels are God's created beings. Also, note that these "sons of god" are not angels, but men who are walking with God, yet choosing daughters of men from the unsaved. It would fit perfectly with what God warned about the righteous having fellowship with the unrighteous as a pattern all throughout the Bible. We need to ask, who are the sons of God? I believe as we read it in context we should see for ourselves: "And the Lord said, My spirit shall not always strive with man, for that he also is flesh: yet his days shall be an hundred and twenty years'" (Gen. 6:3).

As we read this statement, it seems the Lord is saying man's days are 120 years, or the length of his time on Earth until he dies. At this time, men lived much longer than 120 years, and after the flood, those years started to decrease. Job lived to an age of 140 years. It seems most probable that he lived before the time of Moses, after that time the days of human life were much shortened,

Moses is an example of a man who lived to an age of 120 years after the flood according to the Bible: "And Moses was an hundred and twenty years old when he died: his eye was not dim, nor his natural force abated" (Deut. 34:7).

If we study this further, we will find Moses didn't go over the Jordan river into the promised land because he sinned and hit the rock two times, when the Lord told him to just speak to it the second time:

Take the rod, and gather thou the assembly together, thou, and Aaron thy brother, and speak ye unto the rock before their eyes; and it shall give forth his water, and thou shalt bring forth to them water out of the rock: so thou shalt give the congregation and their beasts drink. And Moses took the rod from before the Lord, as he commanded him. And Moses and Aaron gathered the congregation together before the rock, and he said unto them, "Hear now, ye rebels; must we fetch you water out of this rock?" And Moses lifted up his hand, and with his rod he smote the rock twice: and the water came out abundantly, and the congregation drank, and their beasts also. And the Lord spake unto Moses and Aaron, "Because ye believed me not, to sanctify me in the eyes of the children of Israel, therefore ye shall not bring this congregation into the land which I have given them." (Num. 20:8–12)

This shows us that Moses would die before he went into the Promised Land west of the Jordan River (Deut. 31:14). Moses could have lived a little longer if he had not hit the rock the second time.

Over the years, man's age would be seventy years, or eighty years, if by reason of strength, according to Psalm 90:

> The days of our years are threescore years and ten; and if by reason of strength they be fourscore years, yet is their strength labour and sorrow; for it is soon cut off, and we fly away. Who knoweth the power of thine anger? even according to thy fear, so is thy wrath. So teach us to number our days, that we may apply our hearts unto wisdom. (Ps. 90:10–12)

We know today, the average lifespan can be seventy or eighty years, even 100, or past 110, if that person is healthy and comes from good genetic background.

So what could the Lord be saying to Noah about the 120 years?

Think about this: man's civilization, the human race, had only 120 years until judgment was coming because of their wickedness. God had enough.

LAND OF THE GIANTS

"There were giants in the earth in those days; and also after that, when the sons of God came in unto the daughters of men, and they bare children to them, the same became mighty men which were of old, men of renown" (Gen. 6:4).

Reading this last verse, it would seem, "the sons of God came to the daughters of men and they bare children to them, the same became mighty men which were of old."

Were they physically old? No, of course not. But they did become mighty, and were men of renown. In Hebrew,

(Shem) *nenown*, means name, of reputation, fame and glory, memorial, monument.

And "of old" in Hebrew, *owlam*, means ancient time, long time. This understanding of old, is found in Genesis chapter 4, as men gained knowledge, might, and became names of importance to the world by the influence of Satan to corrupt them through the works of their hands.

We read before spirits, or angels, cannot have power to transform themselves into humans to have sex with daughters of men. There is not one Bible verse that supports this idea. That would be a form of *evolution,* which the Bible rejects. Some secular people accept TV programs like Ancient Aliens (from other worlds) that explores the controversial theory that extraterrestrials have visited earth for millions of years.

Can angels transform into flesh and blood?

Notice what the Bible has to say about transformation into another form:

> But God giveth it a body as it hath pleased him, and to every seed his own body. All flesh is not the same flesh: but there is one kind of flesh of men, another flesh of beasts, another of fishes, and another of birds. There are also celestial (upon or above the heavens) bodies, and bodies terrestrial: (belonging to the earth) but the glory of the celestial is one, and the glory of the terrestrial is another. (1 Cor. 15:38–40)

They are separate. "The glory of the celestial is one, and the glory of the terrestrial is another."

If we believe the Bible has the truth, we need to learn *through its wisdom.* We should then believe that there is only one type of seed, or one kind of flesh of men.

We have different sizes, shapes, and heights of humans. Yet nothing suggests that an angel can become human and have sexual intercourse with a woman. Blood and sperm sets things into motion to bring life.

As we study the Bible, we will know the truth. There are other books that some people claim to be the Word of God, such as the book of Enoch, which was written somewhat later, and which some scholars believe to have been written at about 167 BCE. However, most scholars do not know when the book of Enoch was written or who the author was, or that which Jude was quoting had any reference to this book.

The biblical figure Enoch was not the author, but rather, someone who lived closer to the time of Christ, or possibly even after Christ, according to some references. There are many arguments on all sides of this debate, but the real question in many Christian minds is whether it is scriptural.

If an idea does not agree with scripture from the Bible, then we have a red flag. How can we study it? Can I point to the references that support it in other books of the Bible?

This is what Wikipedia had to say about it:

> The Book of Enoch (also 1 Enoch Ge'ez: mets'iḥāfe hēnoki) is an ancient Jewish religious work, ascribed by tradition to Enoch, the great-grandfather of Noah. The older sections (mainly in the Book of the Watchers) of the text are dated from about 300 BCE, and the latest part (Book of Parables) probably to the 1st century BCE.

> It is not part of the biblical canon as used by Jews, apart from Beta Israel. Most Christian denominations and traditions may accept the Books of Enoch as having some historical or theological interest, but they generally regard the Books of Enoch as non-canonical or non-inspired. It is regarded as canonical by the Ethiopian Orthodox Tewahedo Church and

Eritrean Orthodox Tewahedo Church, but not by any other Christian groups.

People use this book to *enforce the theory* that angels became men with flesh and blood. The History Channel presents a program called "Ancient Aliens" that gives the same explanation with the additional viewpoint that they were from another planet.

I must say, this doesn't build my faith. It doesn't support any biblical argument, and we need to be careful about too quickly accepting what so-called experts say.

If we believe that these sons of God were angels that used human women for their desires and then had offspring that were *half-angel and half-human*, then that reasoning of part-angel and part-human creatures results from opinions, and it is a strange concept.

It violates one of the most basic understandings that creationists firmly teach and uphold.

As we study Genesis chapter one, a *strong argument* is made that God only creates things that can only *reproduce after their own kind*.

(Gen. 1:24–27; God explains how he did it in Genesis 2:7 and for Eve in Gen. 2:21–25).

And God said, "Let the earth bring forth the living creature after his kind, cattle, and creeping thing, and beast of the earth after his kind:" and it was so. And God made the beast of the earth after his kind, and cattle after their kind, and every thing that creepeth upon the earth after his kind: and God saw that it was good. And God said, "Let us make man in our image, after our likeness: and let them have dominion over the fish of the sea, and over the fowl of the air, and over the cattle, and over all the earth, and over every creeping thing that creepeth upon the earth." So God created man in his own image, in the image of God created he him; male and female created he them. (Gen. 1:24–27)

"And the Lord God formed man of the dust of the ground, and breathed into his nostrils the breath of life; and man became a living soul" (Gen. 2:7).

And the Lord God caused a deep sleep to fall upon Adam, and he slept: and he took one of his ribs, and closed up the flesh instead thereof; and the rib, which the Lord God had taken from man, made he a woman, and brought her unto the man. And Adam said, "This is now bone of my bones, and flesh of my flesh: she shall be called Woman, because she was taken out of Man. Therefore shall a man leave his father and his mother, and shall cleave unto his wife: and they shall be one flesh. And they were both naked, the man and his wife, and were not ashamed." (Gen. 2:21–25)

Consider the idea of "kind" for a few minutes.

In Hebrew, the word *miyn* means kind; sometimes a species (usually of animals). Groups of living organisms belong in the same created "kind" if they have descended from the same ancestral gene pool. This does not preclude new species because this represents a partitioning of the original gene pool. Information is lost or conserved—not gained. A new species could arise when a population is isolated and inbreeding occurs. By this definition, a new species is not a new "kind" but a further partitioning of an existing "kind" (Strong's Blue letter Concordance to the Bible).

Here are a few scriptures that support this word: Gen. 1:12, 21, 24, 25; 6:20.

The Greek word *physis* means the nature of things, the force, laws, order of nature, birth, physical origin, a mode of feeling and acting which by long habit has become nature; the sum of innate properties and powers by which one person differs from others, distinctive native peculiarities, natural characteristics: the natural strength, ferocity, and intractability of beasts.

"For every kind of beasts, and of birds, and of serpents, and of things in the sea, is tamed, and hath been tamed of mankind" (James 3:7).

Notice what Paul says: "All flesh is not the same flesh: but there is one kind of flesh of men, another flesh of beasts, another of fishes, and another of birds" (1 Cor. 15:39).

Another Greek word is *sarx*, which means flesh (the soft substance of the living body, which covers the bones and is permeated with blood) of both man and beasts. The body of a man used of natural or physical origin, generation or relationship born of natural generation of the sensuous nature of man, "the animal nature."

As we check these references, it indicates that there is one flesh for all creatures. They never exchange their DNA or genes.

Humans and angels are *two entirely different "kinds."* Angels were created as spiritual beings of great power that do not have flesh or blood.

Man (Adam) came directly from the dust of the earth, and Eve came from Adam's rib as we have seen in the Bible. Then they procreated on their own through nature, and God placed a spirit in the embryo (Ps. 139:13–15; Job 10:18; Ps. 22:9; Jer. 1:5).

Evil angels or spirits have a symbolic appearance of unclean animals, birds, and shadows, they can appear like male or females, or angels of light to deceive.

What about these giants? Were there giants in the Bible?

First let's see what this word means in the Bible, and read it in context. The Strong's Blue letter Bible Concordance tells us.

Giants, in Hebrew, is *nĕphiyl*, and means giants, the Nephilim.nef-eel'; or נְפִל nᵉphil; from H5307; properly, a feller, i.e. a bully or tyrant:—giant.

From Nephilim to fall, to lie, be cast down, to fail.

Just as Cain's behavior was against God's ways (Gen. 4:6).

Some see evidence from these scriptures in Numbers 13:32–33 that the Nephilim were giants, referring to their size.

Right here we can read that the Israelite spies went into the Promised Land, and they said they saw the Nephilim who made them appear in their "own eyes as grasshoppers and so we were in their eyes."

This would have brought fear to the people; but there was no encounter with the Nephilim once they entered into the land.

Those of giant size, who were later actually seen, are called Rephaim (Deut. 1:28, 2:11, 20, 9:2). It appears the spies over-exaggerated their incorrect descriptions of these people. Their report was rejected by Moses, and later those spies died because of this report, which brought fear to Israel (Num. 14:1–38).

The name Nephilim comes from the Hebrew verb root *naphal*, meaning "the fallen ones." This brings understanding if we are dealing with intermarriage between believers and unbelievers (or ungodly).

This is what God didn't want either before the flood or after. He knew the problems it would cause among themselves and their children.

The offspring were the result of believers ("sons of God") who fell from the faith by marrying unbelieving, sensual, carnal-minded women. The examples of this are amazing. Remember Samson and Solomon? It brought death and wickedness, because their hearts were seduced by these types of women.

The children were raised in an unscriptural, hostile, anti-God culture. A perfect example is the *pre-flood rebellion* against the Creator Yehweh, which brought their demise.

This has been the pattern and the model for considerable time in the modern world.

Certainly some of the worse enemies of Christianity were brought up in Christian homes or environments that spoke of godly values and then because of rejection, anger, and a lack of self-esteem, these people would turn against God because they saw hypocrisy, or because their questions were not answered. Then Satan would use that instability to deceive them.

They have forsaken the truth of the faith of their parents (that are saved) in order to seek the knowledge and rebellion of the world. Like the ancient heroes before the great Deluge, they have often become powerful examples and instruments in anti-God establishments and views in our culture.

For the same reason God brought about a worldwide flood in Noah's time, God will once again intervene definitely in the future. This time it will be by *universal fire*, destroying the present earth and then creating a New Heaven and a New Earth "wherein dwells righteousness" (2 Pet. 3:13).

> Seeing then that all these things shall be dissolved, what manner of persons ought ye to be in all holy conversation and godliness, looking for and hasting unto the coming of the day of God, wherein the heavens being on fire shall be dissolved, and the elements shall melt with fervent heat? Nevertheless we, according to his promise, look for new heavens and a new earth, wherein dwelleth righteousness. (2 Pet. 3:11–13)

Now back to where we were.

In the Bible, there are only two scriptures using this Hebrew word *Něphiyl*:

"There were giants in the earth in those days; and also after that, when the sons of God came in unto the daughters of men, and they bare children to them, the same became mighty men which were of old, men of renown" (Gen. 6:4).

"And there we saw the giants, the sons of Anak, which come of the giants: and we were in our own sight as grasshoppers, and so we were in their sight" (Num. 13:33).

Who were these people? Were they tall enough that Israel felt they were like grasshoppers? Were they like maybe fifteen, twenty, thirty feet tall?

No, it's a figure of speech. The Bible should not be taken literally at times. As we read it, it will explain itself. Sometimes it is written using symbolism to explain a truth. Other times, it is literal speaking of true events.

We know that King David's opponent was a little over nine feet, which is documented in scripture.

That is the only known scripture that showed the height of the giant of Gath (1 Sam. 17:4) and his sons (2 Sam. 21:15–22; 1 Chron. 20:4–8).

Some say that descendants from the Nephilim were the giants that Israel faced.

Only one problem with that: Noah and his family were not giants. They were the only ones that remained on the earth after the flood, and their descendants were of the same kind, all human.

There were people that were taller and stronger, yet all came from the same kind. *The seed of men.*

The word "giant" doesn't just reveal their size. It can mean their power, ability, technology, or success.

Let's look at the sons of Anak. Hebrew: *Anaq*, Anak = "neck", progenitor of a family, or tribe of the giant people in Canaan.

We know there are tall people and small people in many countries and islands that are remote locations of the world. Yet they are all human, from the seed of man.

Scripture says that after Israel came out of Egypt, Moses sent twelve spies into the land:

> Nevertheless the people be strong (strong, mighty, fierce) that dwell in the land, and the cities are walled, and very great: (large in magnitude and extent, in number) and moreover we saw the children of Anak there. The Amalekites dwell in the land of the south: and the Hittites, and the Jebusites, and the Amorites, dwell in the mountains: and the Canaanites dwell by the sea, and by the coast of Jordan. And Caleb stilled the people before Moses, and said, "Let us go up at once, and possess it; for we are well able to overcome it." But the men that went up with him said, "We be not able to go up against the people; for they are stronger than we." And they brought up an evil report of the land which they had searched unto the children of Israel, saying, "The land, through which we have gone to search it, is a land that eateth up the inhabitants thereof; and all the people that we saw in it are men of a great stature. And there we saw the giants, the sons of Anak, which come of the giants: and we were in our own sight as grasshoppers, and so we were in their sight." (Num. 13:28–33)

This was their report to Moses. Were the people actually as tall as was reported, or did they only appear that way? They were strong, and their cities fortified, and their size was massive. By the accounts of Israel's wars in the Bible, they would seem that way, but not as our imagination suggests or according to what others have said about this theory.

69

We need to examine the scriptures we read, and test every idea and opinion with God's written Word.

The next chapter will cover Genesis 6. We will go into more detail about this generation (Noah's time) and learn that it would be fit for destruction as men and women would contribute to influence this rebellion into their children.

This same behavior would increase in the future to bring about a generation of destruction.

CHILDREN OF REBELLION

—❧—

"There were giants in the earth in those days; and also after that, when the sons of God came in unto the daughters of men, and they bare children to them, the same became mighty men which were of old, men of renown" (Gen. 6:4)

Let's talk about the children that came from the Sons of God (not the angels). The saved men walking with God had relations with the daughters of men, which were unsaved.

This concept agrees with all Scripture, since the beginning of creation. Man would sin and would continue to rebel against God, while others would sin, then repent (change their mind), and come back to God.

Just as Satan tempted Eve by saying, "You shall be as gods, knowing good and evil."

These same thoughts came to Cain, Eve's firstborn, thinking he knew better than God, as shown by his actions. Cain had children, and I'm very sure he didn't teach them the ways of the Lord by what came out of his mouth, nor as shown by his behavior. Cain directed his children by what he endured and suffered, which he thought was an injustice.

The parent has plenty of responsibility to raise up their children correctly because it will influence them for the rest of their lives in one way or another. In this chapter, we will discover that when the parents do not seek after God, it will affect their children, unless they repent and direct their desires toward the Lord's Word.

The parents are an example of what their children will become.

HUSBAND, WIFE, AND COUNSELING

We can see a conflict in this world. If a man or woman desires to walk with God and the spouse doesn't, then wouldn't you think they might not see eye to eye in the situations they face?

Their discussions could be, I would suggest, less agreeable?

Sure, there could be love, respect, and honor, yet there will be that thin line of division from not being on the same page because of different beliefs, ideas, and goals. This can be induced in relationships and that will affect the wife and her children later.

For example, let us talk about the husband and wife. If there is not a healthy relationship of honor and respect toward one another, plus placing God's written Word above themselves, then there are going to be problems developing over the years. Small scars, from hurts, and miscommunications, which have been ignored and maybe forgotten for a while, may be triggered and raised to the surface like a flood.

It's not easy seeing our own problems. It can take someone from the outside that is not taking either side.

The Lord knows us, and He will teach us if we study for an answer in his written Word.

Firstly, not just reading the Bible randomly, but diligently searching for an answer from the scriptures.

Secondly, a good friend that uses wisdom from God's Word can help us.

There are many sources in the church on relationships, and these sources instruct us on how to handle them with good discernment. Check all sources that they are in agreement with the scriptures.

For example, what did Paul the Apostle say? Does God want a saved woman to stay with her husband even if he doesn't believe?

Paul instructs us as follows:

But to the rest speak I, not the Lord: If any brother hath a wife that believeth not, and she be pleased to dwell with him, let him not put her away. And the woman which hath an husband that believeth not, and if he be pleased to dwell with her, let her not leave him. For the unbelieving husband is sanctified by the wife, and the unbelieving wife is sanctified by the husband: else were your children unclean; but now are they holy. But if the unbelieving depart, let him depart. A brother or a sister is not under bondage in such cases: but God hath called us to peace. (1 Cor. 7:12–15)

Paul was sharing what he thought, with his understanding of the scriptures. You have to read the whole chapter to understand why it was written that way.

If the couple stays together, then *it will benefit them and their children*, if they are taught in the ways of the Lord. Now, if there is verbal abuse, then she or he needs to have a third-party help discuss both sides of the situation to seek answers in God's Word to diagnose treatment spiritually.

Sometimes professional advice is helpful, but it is never the cure.

If there is physical abuse, she or he needs to get out of that situation fast, and go to the authorities and then proceed from there.

Yet, I'm speaking of extremes.

We need to take heed to what Paul said about this, about fellowship, and how the woman may stay with her husband, even if he doesn't believe.

A husband might be drawn to Christ through his wife's behavior, her good deeds in Christ, and her pleasant words.

If the couple has children, the children would see a good role model of this healthful behavior in the family, and through peace in the home.

As children of the Lord (spiritually speaking), we should set that example. Both the man and the woman. Then it will pass on to our children.

A quick thought:

Children do have a free will, and they will look at our example of how we present the Gospel. Did we rush them into it, pushing the Bible down their throats, or present it in a peaceful and loving way? And do not forget, there may be other influences outside of the family that may not help to contribute positively to the situation.

God's written Word does reveal sin, righteous, and judgment, so as we search the scriptures we can discover our heart.

We all have shared Bible verses at one time or another with zeal, rather than wisdom. It happens. Don't beat yourself up over it. God will use what you have shared with your children. Also, pray for them. Parents aren't perfect, nor is any earthly counselor that will try to fix your problems. Only Jesus our Lord, his Holy Spirit, and his written Word will bring rest, confidence, peace, understanding, knowledge, and wisdom.

Make sure your counselors—whoever they may be—are spiritually sound. The Bible does say to have more than one. The Bible is filled with people directed by the Holy Ghost and their advice comes at no cost.

Here are some of those scriptures that display counseling:

"For unto us a child is born, unto us a son is given: and the government shall be upon his shoulder: and his name shall be called Wonderful, Counseller, The mighty God, The everlasting Father, The Prince of Peace." (Isa. 9:6)

"Thy testimonies also are my delight and my counsellers." (Ps. 119:24)

"Where no counsel is, the people fall: but in the multitude of counsellers there is safety." (Prov. 11:14)

"Without counsel purposes are disappointed: but in the multitude of counsellers they are established." (Prov. 15:22)

"Also Jonathan David's uncle was a counseller, a wise man, and a scribe: and Jehiel the son of Hachmoni was with the king's sons:" (1 Chron. 27:32)

"The way of a fool is right in his own eyes: but he that hearkeneth unto counsel is wise." (Prov. 12:15)

It would be foolish not to listen to those who are older and experienced from labor in God's Word. Whether we receive good or bad advice, we should be able to take what we hear and then compare it with God's written Word.

"For the word of God is quick (alive), and powerful, and sharper than any two-edged sword, piercing even to the dividing asunder of soul and spirit, and of the joints and marrow, and is a discerner (critic and judge) of the thoughts and intents of the heart" (Heb. 4:12).

They need to hear the matter, both sides of the conversation, with respect and humbleness.

"He that answereth a matter before he heareth it, it is folly and shame unto him" (Prov. 18:13).

"And I myself also am persuaded of you, my brethren, that ye also are full of goodness, filled with all knowledge, able also to admonish one another." (Rom. 15:14)

If we read and study God's Word, it will benefit us more than we can ever imagine. We can grow in faith and can watch how the Lord will work things out, because we are working together with God. We are never alone, even though we may feel like it at times. You can tell others what the Lord has done for both you and those around you.

That is a testimony—a testimony of victory, not defeat.

Before the flood of Noah, we can imagine how the parents and children were behaving, with the evil that was in the world.

There were very few people who stood for the Lord and walked with him. Could it be that same way in the days that are coming? We will see.

THE CHILDREN OF THE TIMES

As we discussed, if the parents are not saved, or only one family member is, that might cause confusion for the children. God has seen this since the beginning; however, he won't force his will on you.

The children that were living in the days of Noah reacted to what they experienced through their family, friends, education, culture, and the worldview in those days. It was very persuasive and seductive. Their behavior would have been corrupted by what was commonly accepted.

The Lord saw the wickedness and rebellion of the parents, which spread to the children, and it corrupted the children.

If you notice, our world is being overturned by every sinful behavior and wicked imagination that can enter into the mind. The world's gospel is, "It should be accepted, because we have rights." Yes, they do have that choice. Yes, they do have a free will.

Should not we also have the right not to agree with worldly behavior, and not for those people to impose their lifestyle down our throats?

I truly believe that the prophets, including the Apostles, wrote of our times and our future. We know there was wickedness back then, and they had all sorts of problems.

Yet, not at the scale we have noticed since this generation began. You might say cable television, the internet, and social media have contributed to ruining morality and accountability.

Sure, there are some good things, and they are helpful for business, education, socializing, and sharing the love of God with people across the seas and in our own land. Yet many are angry, insecure, victim-minded people that cannot wait to tell you their story, not looking for help, but to complain and fight with others by protest, or online when they don't agree with others. They now have that opportunity to be noticed.

At times children have no idea what they are doing or why they do it. Cunningly designed indoctrination coming in from all areas influence their minds. Our children are tempted through every sexual idea from advertising, cable media, movies, music, and videos, plus even our schools can have this influence.

Children have their own phones that are unsupervised and are becoming "i-kids" (a new term for children with iPhones). Parents need to pay careful attention to what their children are watching. It is not uncommon for children from the ages of five and six years old to have their own phones. That's our culture: *"the age of the selfie."* Schools may contribute to the problem, when they have the mindset of far-left extreme liberalism and self-indulgence, which will cause many types of mental disorders with confusion, entangled in intolerance and narcissism (which really shows pride, according to scripture).

Consider the word "intolerant" for a few minutes.

From the Webster Dictionary:

Not tolerant of views, beliefs, or behavior that differ from one's own.

"he was intolerant of ignorance"

synonyms: bigoted, narrow-minded, small-minded, parochial, provincial, insular, blinkered, illiberal, inflexible, dogmatic, rigid, uncompromising, unforgiving, unsympathetic; prejudiced, biased, partial, partisan, one-sided, sectarian, discriminatory, unfair, unjust.

To make this simple, if you disagree with someone on the left, you can be placed on a list. They will see you as a hateful, bigoted, unsympathetic person, and not loving.

That's how the "far left" will see you *if you disagree with them*. As a matter of fact, if you agree with God's written Word, you will already be judged in word and deed.

Our children are seduced by more far left liberal lifestyles that oppose common sense, than by honest biblical behaviors. The world is setting the standards of morality, relationships, love, and acceptance without excuse and without retreat.

Our children become undisciplined, demanding, insecure, immature, aggressive, miserable spoiled children. They become selfish, not thinking of anyone's needs but their own. They feel entitled, and they claim that you owe it to them.

They don't ask, but demand to have it their way, from grade school to college, and beyond that. Because of fears and wounds in their life, they become this way and that allows the devil to seduce them, lie to them, and bring accusations against them. They become over sensitive, not willing to hear a conversation, or to have a civil discussion.

The technological age has contributed to this situation also, and is used by parents that allow the child to grow mentally on their own. Indulgent parents let kids "rule their own world." *Kids are being trained-up* with a sense of *entitlement, rather than responsibility and accountability*. This lifestyle creates inadequate sleep patterns, unbalanced nutrition, low physical skills, and no ability to handle rejection because of low self-esteem. *Children become resistant to correction and instruction.*

All these are factors that change our children into mindless "robots."

Consider what the Lord said through Paul:

"Wherefore be ye not unwise (without a mind), but understanding what the will (wish or will) of the Lord is" (Eph. 5:17).

Unwise (in Greek: *aphrōn*) means "without a mind", senseless, foolish, stupid.

The Lord is telling us to use the brain he gave us, and to learn his will, and his will is found in his written Word (Rom. 12:1–2).

This is the peace and rest that we need to calm our mind and spirit.

Concerning children, we see that a desk-bound indoor lifestyle is harming our children and they are not receiving enough exercise or personal contacts. This is not helping their social skills, or helping them handle opposition in a healthful way, in which we all are accustomed. It's not helping their growth in friendships, or their identity and desire to be more responsible and accountable.

Long-time exposure to iPhones and video games will bring inadequate sleep and unbalanced nutrition. You can check that out for yourself and see it in the behavior of your children. Endless stimulation brings a world of fantasy, preconceived desires, and wishes that can hinder real life activities and responsibilities. *It can numb the senses and cause a person become indifferent. Kids become lazy.*

"Indifferent", from Webster, means: Indifferent, unconcerned, incurious, aloof, detached, disinterested mean not showing or feeling interest. Indifferent implies neutrality of attitude from lack of inclination, preference, or prejudice.

It's a technological babysitter. This isn't a good idea without supervision. It's our job to *raise our child.*

No one should have that power over them. Not even schools. Whoever teaches children will influence them, and the children will be brought up in their standards. By the way, if they have problems—mental, physical, or spiritual—the children can learn where to find help from their parents' instruction, *if the parents are seeking answers in God's Word*. Not just a little Bible study, but seriously seeking the truth in which their children will grow.

If you do not study and read God's Word, then you might have problems raising your children. How can you truly teach them correctly? With the truth. Show them that God's ways are much better, more powerful, and more restful than the world's philosophies. Help them learn how to love and to live life with knowledge and wisdom, *to love correction and instruction* as a part of growing up and building one's character in Christ.

If you feed, clothe, and provide for your children, then you love them. Websites, movies, and games are not always looking out for our best interests. They are just entertaining us. It's a quick fix, like a drug. "Instant gratification." Remember that old saying: "If it feels good, do it"?

Children are taught by others from what they experience, and from what they see, hear, and feel. Their brains are forming and are being filled with ideas from whomever is teaching them. They are being indoctrinated and fashioned by these opinions, lifestyles, and cultures.

What is revealed to children, attracts their curiosity. With this behavior growing within them, they will desire to become more entertained, seeking to satisfy those desires. If not met in the time they want, dissatisfaction comes and a lack of peace and rest manifests in them. Then they become like protesters when you try to counsel them.

They are not aware of it, yet they know something is wrong. Deep down within themselves they need to fill that hole. They need to feel fulfilled, happy, and safe.

This is when *instant gratification* seems to be their answer.

Gratification means pleasure, especially when gained from the satisfaction of desire-fulfillment, indulgence, relief, or appeasement.

It seems that we first want to be pleased, rather than thinking about pleasing others and God. Children cannot help it because they are young and are dependent on their parents. The manner in which they are taught is going to do two things:: either they will receive what they are taught, or they will rebel against it.

We live in a sexual society, it's everywhere. I don't have to tell you this.

You and your kids are the target, and Satan and his devils will not give up. We live in a world that gives you imaginations about what you want to be. There are no rules or guidelines with the increasing rise of *self-identification*.

The reality is the secular world is against God's teachings.

Even the common teaching of biology. God created a person to be *either male or female*. That's it. It's not my opinion. God created nature, which he started from the beginning. Get mad at God if you disagree with him. I wouldn't suggest that as a course of action, if I were you.

Yet feelings within make you feel that you aren't the person you should be.

Psychologists (people who study the human mind, human emotions, and behavior) and far-left liberal teachers in the education system, parents, social activities, movies, media, and other lifestyles all combat each other and cause confusion in the mind of a child whose *brain is developing*. Also, do not forget unclean demonic influences. (See *Spiritual Warfare: The Battle Continues*, my fourth book, by the grace of God.)

What it accomplishes is this: it destroys the identity of who you truly are and how nature made you by your parents through God's laws of procreation.

We are *either male or female* by the proof of genetics. According to genetics, the sex of an individual is determined by a pair of sex chromosomes. Females typically have two of the same kind of sex chromosomes (XX), and they are called the homogametic sex. Males typically have two different kinds of sex chromosomes (XY) and are called the heterogametic sex.

Human physiology is the study of how the human body functions. This includes the mechanical, physical, bioelectrical, and biochemical functions of humans in good health, from the organs to the cells of which they are composed. The human body consists of many interacting systems of organs.

Biology: the study of living organisms is divided into many specialized fields that cover their morphology, physiology, anatomy, behavior, origin, and distribution.

We cannot ignore this. We cannot ignore how a person feels about oneself, and what they have heard or experienced. Illegitimate lifestyles can become very dangerous, both physically and mentally.

The suicide rate among teenagers is very high. Suicide is the second leading cause of death among teenagers, according to different reports in media.

Suicide can be the result of depression, injury, poisoning, or overdose. Teenagers have attempted suicide because of family rejection in their life, plus the confusion, fear and anxiety of what is going on in their head.

This isn't what God wanted. God will never impose his views on us. He loves us, warns us, and tries to teach us. Our country and others are *leading this sexual revolution.* If it feels good, do it. That is the message: be who you are.

We just don't know or realize the consequences, and how it's going to affect the rest of our lives. If we're not saved, it will negatively affect our life to come. We don't need to point a self-righteous finger thinking they are worse than us. We all have sinned, and *we all need a savior*.

> For God so loved the world, that he gave his only begotten Son, that whosoever believeth in him should not perish, but have everlasting life. For God sent not his Son into the world to condemn the world; but that the world through him might be saved. He that believeth on him is not condemned: but he that believeth not is condemned already, because he hath not believed in the name of the only begotten Son of God. (John 3:16–18)

God doesn't care for our lifestyles or choices; he loves us and wants to free us from ourselves, and from the common view of the world, plus demonic influence. God set the rules, not us. He is the one who defined sin, and out of his love and mercy, God provided a remedy for sin—all sin. *It's through repentance (to change the mind) and faith in His Son Jesus Christ, who paid for our sins.*

Marriage between the same sexes brings rejection, confusion, and dread. The family unit of a mother and father is no longer seen as God wanted since the beginning (according to the book of Genesis). This creates deep rejection and insecurity, no matter how much one denies it. It brings a mental imbalance for extreme desires that cause people to reject a person and to disconnect physically and mentally. We must learn along with our kids not to have it our way; not to be selfish or self-centered, but to give our hearts to God and those around us, seeking how we may help them. Not seeking our will, but God's, by learning his written Word and through fellowship and knowing our *authority and ability* over the devil.

If we don't treat this problem with God's Word by talking to our children and properly instructing them, we will pay for it later as they grow up.

Matthew wrote this on true love:

> Jesus said unto him, "Thou shalt love the Lord thy God with all thy heart, and with all thy soul, and with all thy mind. This is the first and great commandment. And the second is like unto it, 'Thou shalt love thy neighbour as thyself.' On these two commandments hang all the law and the prophets." (Matt. 22:37–40)

We need to reveal that love to our children through truth and knowledge with wisdom from the scriptures. They may not like it or agree, yet that's our responsibility. *If you love them,* you will show them by your works and behavior.

Paul had something to say to Timothy on unhealthful behavior, and how we can grow in knowledge and we can compare it to today:

> O Timothy, keep (watch, keep watch, observe) that which is committed to thy trust, avoiding profane (to turn off or aside, lawful to be trodden (like to crush)) and vain babblings (empty discussion, discussion of vain and useless matters), and oppositions of science (gnōsis, knowledge) falsely so called: Which some professing have erred (miss the mark) concerning the faith (steadfastness). Grace be with thee. Amen. (1 Tim. 6:20–21)

Our children are being taught the ways of the world. Everything from eating, drinking, lifestyles, and choices. They are bombarded from every direction—from cable, smartphones, and any type of electronic device.

What they watch and read is teaching them what is acceptable, true, pure, fun, exciting, and adventurous. To try new things and explore thoughts in which they are indoctrinated. If our children know the Lord, even their church could be providing the wrong environment if it is guilty of a *far-left liberal indoctrination* that opposes the truth of scriptures. At times, the modern church is against good old-fashioned common sense.

The battle is real. More believers in Christ can see it. Yet we are never alone, even if we feel the weight of the nonsense, stupidity, and the lack of fundamental common sense that is ignored.

Do not forget that the devil could be speaking to them about what they experience through their influences.

We are not alone. As we trust in God's written Word, he will help us and teach us.

We are victors, not victim-minded.

"There hath no temptation taken you but such as is common to man: but God is faithful, who will not suffer you to be tempted above that ye are able; but will with the temptation also make a way to escape, that ye may be able to bear it" (1 Cor. 10:13).

We can take control of our thoughts.

(For the weapons of our warfare are not carnal, but mighty through God to the pulling down of strong holds) Casting down imaginations (reasoning) and every high thing that exalteth itself against the knowledge of God, and bringing into captivity every thought to the obedience of Christ; and having in a readiness to revenge all disobedience, when your obedience is fulfilled. (2 Cor. 10:4–6)

God makes it simple; we make it difficult. If you ever study this, and all these points, you will be healthier, happier, and blessed in your mind and spirit.

As parents, we will go through these temptations just as our children will.

We must take notice and be involved with our children. Don't be some type of dictator, but in love and wisdom instruct your children in what you want. Listen to your children with an understanding heart; yet, you are the parent, not your children.

Our children are going through temptations, just as we are. Watch for the warning signs, not in fear, but be in a restful state of mind, filled with peace and trust as you are seeking God's guidance through his written Word.

Take the problems that you are facing to Psalms and Proverbs, and to the words of Jesus and his servants in the Bible.

That is the best advice, and it costs nothing.

Parents need to learn God's written Word, not just for their own sake, but also for the sake of their children likewise. We do not have to be overbearing, but should be gentle to help them understand what is right and wrong. You guide them and teach them.

As they become older, give them space, but be firm. Let that love for them be seen by works, not just words, listening to them, understanding them, and asking questions to get them to think.

Then if they have no answer, you can share God's truth with them, because that's when they will listen. Kids don't like long lectures from your wisdom. Wait on God for when to do it. Keep to the point.

This displays God's Word by your actions. Your steadfastness, which is faith, will reveal to them that you are strong in the Lord. Not just telling them and acting like you're holy and righteous. God's Word should be displayed by your actions and confidence. Yes, your lifestyle will play a very important role.

It is very important not to ignore them when they talk or to ignore their behavior.

There is always a root to the problem, which they are unable to see. Yet, God's Word can find that root, expose it, pull it out, and heal them.

It takes time and patience with all of those who are involved.

This next subject is not a popular subject, but we should discuss it.

Suicide: with all the pressures kids go through these days—at school, bullying, home life, and the environment they're in, plus social acceptance and sexual preference—the weight comes down like a load of bricks, and they have no idea why or from where this pressure comes. The stress builds to such levels, they don't know where to turn to or in whom to trust.

One particular gentleman has much to say on this topic. I do not have his site, but I have heard of his name. What he has to say is very interesting and we can learn something from it.

Many people have studied the subject of mental health, and for believers in Christ, it's important to understand it. Better yet, we have the cure through Jesus' wisdom, deliverance, and counsel when we are diligent in seeking the truth through the Holy Ghost and the scriptures.

"They say there is a growing trend of smartphone selfies linked to mental health conditions that focus on a person's behavior. That obsession is with personal appearance: 'our looks,'" according to psychiatrist, Dr. David Veal. He has patients who come to him. The name of the disorder is Body Dysmorphic Disorder (from Webster: a mental disorder characterized by distorted body image and obsessions about perceived physical shortcomings). Since the invention and use of camera phones, teenagers have a compulsion to repeatedly take "selfies" and post them on social media locations and send them to one another.

Dr. Veal has tried different methods to correct the problem. Information can be found anywhere under this subject.

Dr. David Veal continues, "Cognitive behavioral therapy is used to help a patient recognize the reasons for his or her compulsive behavior and then to learn how to work with it and how to moderate the behavior."

This problem has been seen in cases such as teenagers not being completely happy with their "selfies", or the even in the matter of losing weight. Here are a few I found:

A British male teenager tried to commit suicide after he failed to take the perfect selfie.

He became so obsessed with capturing the perfect shot that he spent ten hours a day taking up to two hundred selfies. The nineteen-year-old lost nearly thirty pounds, dropped out of school, and did not leave the house for six months in his quest to get the right picture. He would take ten pictures immediately after waking up. Frustrated at his attempts to take the one image he wanted, he eventually tried to take his own life by overdosing, but was saved by his mom.

The teenager is believed to be the UK's first selfie addict and has had therapy to treat his technology addiction as well as OCD (Obsessive Compulsive Disorder) and Body Dysmorphic Disorder.

"The selfies people take often frequently trigger views of self-indulgence or attention-seeking social dependence that raises the behavior of narcissism or very low self-esteem because of feeling rejection. This action is acted upon excessively and automatically by impulse," said Dr. David Veal.

Narcissistic behavior places enormous pressure on people to achieve unreachable goals that will never be satisfied. The victim becomes withdrawn to a point of depression because of his failures. *Narcissistic behavior is extremely self-centered* with an exaggerated sense of self-importance: it involves protection of one's identity.

It is driven by excessive hero worship, admiration of or infatuation with oneself as a demi-god; to be a wannabe diva. *This diva behavior is very interesting.*

From Webster, the history and etymology for diva: Italian, literally, goddess; from Latin, feminine of divus, divine, god, more at deity.

A famous and successful woman who is very attractive and fashionable, especially: an attractive and successful female performer or celebrity.

The word "God" in Greek, as well in Hebrew, is used many times as an object of worship.

What is worship? It's where we place our time, love, desires, and money. This excessive concern with one's own physical appearance will cause disappointments and disorders that will result in not eating, withdrawing, or overdoing it in exercise. Self-improvement desires can cause one to search for other religions and philosophies, or may lead to substance abuse, which causes harm to our body and conscience.

Here is a list of emotional behavioral changes: egocentric, egoistic (also egoistical), egomaniacal, egotistic (or egotistical), self-absorbed, self-centered, self-concerned, self-infatuated, self-interested, self-involved, self-loving, self-obsessed, self-oriented, self-preoccupied, self-regarding, self-seeking, self-serving, selfish, solipsistic.

Kids have role models, which is common in every generation. Role models can be moderate to extreme. A goal or desire to be a singer, an actor, or an athlete takes plenty of work, and is a desire and influence from the time of one's youth. They see the success and the fantasy. Yet when one is not prepared to work hard to achieve a goal, it is better to lower one's aspirations, than setting up oneself for a fall.

Online manifestations of narcissism may be little more than a self-strategy to validate your self-importance in this world to compensate for a very low and unreliable self-esteem behavior.

These efforts are reinforced and rewarded by other people online. They maintain the distortion of reality in their heads, which creates a brief fantasy of narcissistic delusions, and these are reinforced when *Satan focuses on you*. This deception draws one away from reality and the truth of God's written Word.

The addiction to selfies has also alarmed health professionals. The addiction is influenced by who sees, and who likes, or comments on them. Hoping to reach the greatest number of "likes" is a symptom of the problem that "selfies" are causing. Does the selfie show your worth?

Does God think, "Wow, that is impressive, you are really loved and needed. Look at all the 'likes' you have."

From what I have read and heard, some doctors believe that these behaviors could generate brain problems in the future, especially those related to lack of confidence, insecurity, and rejection.

The word "selfie" was elected "Word of the Year 2013" by the Oxford English Dictionary. It is defined as "a photograph that one has taken of oneself, typically with a smartphone or webcam, and uploaded to a social media website."

I am not saying you should stop this, but don't allow it to control you. You need to control it. Anything can become obsessive.

Paul wrote this to Timothy:

> Charge them that are rich in this world, that they be not high-minded, nor trust in uncertain riches, but in the living God, who giveth us richly all things to enjoy; that they do good, that they be rich in good works, ready to distribute, willing to communicate; laying up in store for themselves a good foundation against the time to come, that they may lay hold on eternal life. (1 Tim. 6:17–19)

We don't need to be high-minded (prideful), or think or place ourselves over others.

What we do in word or deed toward others and ourselves should be what Christ taught, along with the Holy Ghost, and we need to use good common sense.

God gave us a brain; we need to use it rightly, and not to allow things to control us.

We need to seek *God in humbleness and demonstrate grace to all His servants.*

And take heed to yourselves, lest at any time your hearts be overcharged (loaded burdened) with surfeiting (headaches), and drunkenness, and cares (distractions) of this life, and so that day come upon you unawares. For as a snare shall it come on all them that dwell on the face of the whole earth. Watch ye therefore, and pray always, that ye may be accounted worthy to escape all these things that shall come to pass, and to stand before the Son of man. (Luke 21:34–36)

If your eyes are open, our world is getting crazier. It cannot go on like this forever with one part of society opposing God's written Word concerning what He said about how we should live. What will be the consequences? We will bring these problems on ourselves; we can't blame God.

Consider what King Solomon said: "But ye have set at nought all my counsel (advice), and would none of my reproof (correction)."

This is very important. Notice it says "all of his advice". Not some, but all. They didn't take heed to, or pay attention to, his correction. Keep this in mind as we read.

"I also will laugh at your calamity; I will mock when your fear cometh; When your fear cometh as desolation, and your destruction cometh as a whirlwind; when distress and anguish cometh upon you."

(Note: If we reject his advice, which builds our faith, fear will come and that which comes with it.)

"Then shall they call upon me, but I will not answer; they shall seek me early, but they shall not find me: For that they hated knowledge, and did not choose the fear of the Lord."

(This is the answer they hated, which means to oppose his knowledge, which is a part of the fear (reverence) of the Lord.)

"They would none of my counsel: they despised all my reproof. Therefore shall they eat of the fruit of their own way, and be filled with their own devices."

(This reveals that we bring this on ourselves, not the Lord or the devil. We are our worst enemy at times.)

"For the turning away of the simple shall slay them, and the prosperity of fools shall destroy them. But whoso hearkeneth unto me shall dwell safely (confidence), and shall be quiet (ease, secure) from fear of evil." (Prov. 1:25–33)

It is such an easy answer because the Lord wants us to understand. He will teach us and show us, if we are willing.

TRAIN A CHILD IN THE WAY HE SHOULD GO

Our world is changing drastically from what Jesus taught us through his written Word. To live peaceful and quite lives as best as possible, we need to understand how to react, just as his disciples did (1 Tim. 2:1–6).

Romans 12:18 says, "If it be possible, as much as lieth in you, live peaceably with all men."

Many studies have been done on behavior, and books that discuss the behavioral changes in our culture and society have been written.

In this country, everyone has the right and privilege to do whatever they desire, according to the laws.

However this doesn't mean that "as believers" we should agree with these actions or support them. That's our right, and God gives us a free will to make that decision.

Children are the foundation of any nation. What they experience from their youth and the education they receive will cause them to become what they are taught. Even if they rebel against the orthodox instruction of their parents, they will pick and choose from what seems best in their eyes, or what they were indoctrinated. The media (all types) and so-called professionals of psychology (which is the scientific study of the mind and behavior patterns based upon opinions), and psychologists all have their own suggestions for medications and from psychological theory.

Psychology has many sub-fields of study, such as human development, sports, health, clinical, social behavior, and cognitive operation. It's based on practice, observation, and conversations with patients to learn to understand the deep roots that are hidden in life that must be brought to the surface for healing, with the assistance of medical records and human development.

Children need to be taught the truth of God's Word, and by the example that you are displaying. Children's brains are developing as they become older, and they can become easily influenced.

Think of *five main people* in their life, who are their major influences and are whom they will model and imitate.

The Bible shows clearly how to instruct, encourage, and bring up our children. I am sure you can find information from other writers, and by studying your Bible.

We should instruct and correct our children to be gentle and patient with love and grace. This comes with correction and instruction set by our own example and by learning the truth of what is right and wrong.

We should never abuse or hurt, physically or mentally, any child. Yes, at times they need to know what is right and wrong, and a little spanking when they are acting up uncontrollably and stubbornly does remind them that you are the parent.

However, this type of correction isn't always needed. Learn what they want, *and speak with them, not at them*. Always show love, concern, and mercy. Learn to ask them questions because sometimes they feel by their emotions, and they are trying to get your attention in the only way they know how to, by acting up.

Build them up with truth and with civil rewards, and so teach the child that when we do well, we are rewarded. When we do wrong, we must pay for that wrong. This will teach them *accountability and responsibility for their actions*. It will speak to their heart as they get older, even when they act up. Remember, they are not perfect, and neither are we. Work with them, as our Lord works with us with patience.

Below are scriptures that give us instructions on how we should raise our children: "Train up a child in the way he should go: and when he is old, he will not depart from it" (Prov. 22:6).

"And ye shall teach them your children, speaking of them when thou sittest in thine house, and when thou walkest by the way, when thou liest down, and when thou risest up" (Deut. 11:19).

Children, obey your parents in the Lord: for this is right. Honour thy father and mother (which is the first commandment with promise); That it may be well with thee, and thou mayest live long on the earth. And, ye fathers, provoke not your children to wrath: but bring them up in the nurture and admonition of the Lord. (Eph. 6:1–4)

"Correct thy son, and he shall give thee rest; yea, he shall give delight unto thy soul" (Prov. 29:17).

"Fathers, provoke not your children (to anger), lest they be discouraged" (Col. 3:21).

"That they may teach the young women to be sober, to love their husbands, to love their children" (Titus 2:4).

That gives us an idea of how we should bring up our children. Not to hurt them in any way, but to prepare them to be respectful, honorable, responsible, and accountable, as they become adults.

We are drawing near the days that the prophets spoke about (which is what I believe), and we will see changes in this world that we will not desire nor want. It will bring anger, disappointment, frustration and, disgust.

Fear will make us uncomfortable, and create a lack of trust in the Lord that he will provide for or protect us. There is a rise of many mental disorders and depression that affects ourselves as well as our children.

Children do not know who they are. Self-modification of their identity is being inflamed and influenced by wicked spirits, and by all sorts of people.

The world can only place a bandage on it. They can only give a hug or a word of encouragement, group therapy, positive thinking tools, physiological medical assistance for the mental, and medications to ease or to offer some relief. However, *this will never heal you*. Many honest people in those fields will admit that truth.

JESUS IS THE GREAT PHYSICIAN AND THE WONDERFUL COUNSELOR

"For unto us a child is born, unto us a son is given: and the government shall be upon his shoulder: and his name shall be called Wonderful, Counsellor, The mighty God, The everlasting Father, The Prince of Peace" (Isa. 9:6).

We must remember that what Jesus said builds faith, hope, and love: "These things I have spoken unto you, that in me ye might have peace. In the world ye shall have tribulation: but be of good cheer; I have overcome the world" (John 16:33).

When we read Genesis 6 about the behavior and the sins people had, it is important to note that these were the days before the flood. The days of their coming destruction. A generation was destroying itself from within by rejecting God's ways and opinions, and seeking their own desires and pleasures.

The Bible teaches that any sexual behavior besides that of a man and woman within the covenant of marriage is sinful behavior. These writings are proven over thousands of years, yet humans choose what they feel, want, and desire.

We all have sinned. We all can agree with that. This includes premarital sex, extramarital affairs, plus lustful thoughts that are acted out.

This isn't to point a finger at one group or groups. The fact is that all have sinned and fallen short of the glory of God. If we all have sinned, we all need God's mercy and forgiveness.

> Even the righteousness of God which is by faith of Jesus Christ unto all and upon all them that believe: for there is no difference: For all have sinned, and come short of the glory of God; Being justified freely by his grace through the redemption that is in Christ Jesus: Whom God hath set forth to be a propitiation through faith in his blood, to declare his righteousness for the remission of sins that are past, through the forbearance of God; To declare, I say, at this time his righteousness: that he might be just, and the justifier of him which believeth in Jesus. (Rom. 3:22–26)

God wants us to learn his ways, not ours, because our ways will fail sooner or later.

This chapter should give helpful encouragement and a warning to seek after God's ways by the example of what the people faced both before the flood and after.

God's way is "Jesus", by bringing up ourselves and our children in the Lord.

So Shall Also the Coming
of the Son of Man

—⚏—

The chapter in the Bible from where this verse came is very interesting. Matthew 24:37: "But as the days of Noah were, so shall also the coming of the Son of man be." There are many opinions that churches teach differently on the scriptures leading up to this verse.

It would take a series of books to cover just the most common opinions on the precepts and principles in God's Word on the tribulation, the snatching away of the saints (known as the Rapture), leading up to Jesus' second coming, and so on.

Many would throw in their thoughts and give their view that Jesus' second coming was fulfilled already, or that it's symbolic, or biblical events yet to be fulfilled in the future, or many say we just can't know about Jesus' second coming.

These are points that compare the world back then to the world we have today, and to see if there is any similarity in these times, and the importance of understanding our spiritual warfare.

As the writer of this book, I have the burden of presenting to you, the reader, how to search out these things validly. We all seek God's will and prayerfully want to understand God's written Word through our diligence and our desire to learn. Yet many people, for one reason or another, give an excuse by asking, "Where is his coming?"

WHERE IS HIS COMING?

Jesus was telling his disciples about many events that were coming because they asked him questions. At times, Jesus spoke clearly; other times, Jesus spoke in parables. He knew what man could handle, and he knew they would forget what he said until after his resurrection.

"These things understood not his disciples at the first: but when Jesus was glorified, then remembered they that these things were written of him, and that they had done these things unto him" (John 12:16).

The days of Noah is just one of those points. Additionally, Jesus knew all things that he said would be fulfilled in the future.

How far into the future, is the question.

At times, we feel there is a mystery to God, as generation after generation continues without any major manifestation of his display or power as seen by the world.

Humans continue to be complacent with tireless competition in their lives, while people seek their own will, and not wanting to be distracted by their daily activities, being instructed by their professors, teachers, and men of great wisdom, on how to reach their dreams.

With privileges at the feet of those to whom these privileges are granted, schooling and education can be used to better oneself. Yet one's *true education* is being neglected. To understand man is truly nothing, but rather that God should play a major part in their life. *That is truly beneficial.* To come to the understanding that man is here today and gone tomorrow, like a faded flower, as the Bible says.

God himself had a plan, not just for their redemption, but to warn them that he always keeps his word and his prophecies because he loves them, and desires that none perish.

They will say, "Where is your God? I will believe it when I see it."

At God's appointed time, he will answer their requests. Peter wrote these words as directed by the spirit:

This second epistle, beloved, I now write unto you; in both which I stir up your pure minds by way of remembrance: That ye may be mindful of the words which were spoken before by the holy prophets, and of the commandment of us the apostles of the Lord and Saviour: Knowing this first, that there shall come in the last days scoffers, walking after their own lusts, And saying, Where is the promise of his coming? for since the fathers fell asleep, all things continue as they were from the beginning of the creation. For this they willingly are ignorant of, that by the word of God the heavens were of old, and the earth standing out of the water and in the water: Whereby the world that then was, being overflowed with water, perished: But the heavens and the earth, which are now, by the same word are kept in store, reserved unto fire against the day of judgment and perdition of ungodly men. (2 Pet. 3:1–7)

In their unrepentant minds, nothing has changed. The sun comes up, and it goes back down. The seasons come and go. Birth, childhood, youth, adulthood, then old age and death. Those that are rich and those who are not, in many aspects, live out their lives similarly.

We come to this degree of enlightenment (to be wise) that our current time is one of an advanced society, even with the problems we have. Man, for the most part, is civilized—at least that's what they tell us.

People think in their hearts that they do not need to be troubled by myths and fairytales from the past, from the ignorance and superstitions of men. They say it's time to advance and to keep an open mind on what lays ahead in the name of science and education. The rational mind becomes irrational through theory and worldview opinions.

People want to establish their own greatness, magnificence, and intelligence. *To be like a god.* Do these ideas sound familiar?

This is only a part of that sin that caused the flood to come in the days of Noah. If God warned those people through Noah, will he also warn us? We shall see.

Noah was a unique person just before the flood commenced. Only Noah was found to be faithful and blameless among all the earth's people. This is what the Bible tells us, and this is what set him apart from the rest of the people. It was his faith in what God had spoken. We can tell he sought after God on a daily basis. When Noah first heard the words of God, he certainly didn't forget them: "By faith Noah, being warned of God of things not seen as yet, moved with fear, prepared an ark to the saving of his house; by the which he condemned the world, and became heir of the righteousness which is by faith" (Heb. 11:7).

The early verses of Genesis 6, when studied with the rest of the Bible, speak of the faith that had declined in the believing community in the pre-flood times.

Peter gives us some insight:

For Christ also hath once suffered for sins, the just for the unjust, that he might bring us to God, being put to death in the flesh, but quickened by the Spirit: By which also he went and preached unto the spirits in prison; Which sometime were disobedient, when once the longsuffering of God waited in the days of Noah, while the ark was a preparing, wherein few, that is, eight souls were saved by water. (1 Pet. 3:18–20)

THREE THINGS TO THINK ABOUT:

1. Were Noah and his family saved by the water, or by the ark that protected them? They were saved by God warning them of a coming flood, which was the flood of water that killed everything that was not in the ark. This salvation (to keep sound, safe, and at ease) was to preserve their physical lives. Peter speaks of baptism (consecration, placed into) as an example or figure of Christ. We are "placed into" Christ at salvation when we receive him. Then water baptized once we believe.

The like figure whereunto even baptism doth also now save us (not the putting away of the filth of the flesh, but the answer of a good conscience toward God) by the resurrection of Jesus Christ: Who is gone into heaven, and is on the right hand of God; angels and authorities and powers being made subject unto him. (1 Pet. 3:21–22)

What saves us is "the answer of a *good conscience toward God*, by the *resurrection of Jesus Christ*."

2. After Christ died on the cross, his spiritual soul went into paradise, which was in the earth. This is where those who had died then waited to be released after the resurrection of Christ. See my book, *Beyond Paradise*; it covers the details in scripture about their salvation, and ours, in Christ.

In those days, men of God over-desired worldly, unconverted women, and fell from the faith. This problem is still very much with us today. (It likewise occurs with godly women.)

3. Jesus preached to the spirits of those who died in the flood that received God's salvation through faith when they trusted in the blood animal sacrifices, which was God's way of salvation in the Old Testament.

Ephesians tells us:

"Wherefore he saith, When he ascended up on high, he led captivity captive, and gave gifts unto men."

(Note: one gift that Jesus could give was salvation, because they believed.)

"Now that he ascended, what is it but that he also descended first into the lower parts of the earth? He that descended is the same also that ascended up far above all heavens, that he might fill all things" (Eph.4:8–10).

Throughout the Bible, God warns his people through his written Word, not to allow unbelievers to lead them into carnal pursuits and ungodly living.

This was also the major problem of ancient Israel. Kings and prophets faced the same temptations. They continually mixed in the pagan religions of the nations around them, until God had to expel them from the Land of Israel. This included not obeying the sabbaticals that God commanded for their land to rest. This is why the New Testament continues to teach this with utmost importance, for Jesus Christ is *our salvation and rest*.

Before the Flood, godly men chose to marry whomever they wanted, even unbelievers. *This apostasy from the faith* was catastrophic for the morals of the day, and eventually led to a society so corrupt that every thought of their hearts was only evil continually.

The world became a place filled with violence and hatred against God, and was exactly the opposite of the will of the Creator. It was a cesspool of different behaviors, over-desires, lusts, imaginations, and opinions that brought nothing but sin and rebellion against God's will. God's only solution was *total destruction* of all humanity, except for Noah and his immediate family.

In the New Testament, Jesus gave this warning in love, written by Matthew. It would be wise to study what he said:

But as the days of Noah were, so shall also the coming of the Son of man be. For as in the days that were before the flood they were eating and drinking, marrying and giving in marriage, until the day that Noe entered into the ark, And knew not until the flood came, and took them all away; so shall also the coming of the Son of man be. (Matt. 24:37–39)

There are plenty of spiritual revelations and historical events, from the past, to which the scriptures above refer. The Bible covers this in detail.

To understand our warfare and how this relates to back then (by comparing the scriptures to what we see today) is very interesting. We need to be prepared, having the knowledge on how to handle the world with God's wisdom and not our own.

Christ Jesus predicted how the world would become before His return: "*like in the days of Noah*" (Matt. 24:37).

Those days were characterized by the children of God marrying outside of their faith (to unbelievers in Noah's time). Other things also we will cover later.

In God's eyes, this action was seen as violent, as an anti-God rebellion, a society worshiping themselves and not truly understanding who or what they truly were worshiping. Satan was blinding them through their ignorance, using their desires to sway them.

It is not recorded in Genesis 6 that there were massive wars or any details concerning the violence, so we can only imagine. We are told what God saw, as we read the passages of scripture: "And God saw that the wickedness of man was great in the earth, and that every imagination of the thoughts of his heart was only evil continually" (Gen. 6:5).

Solomon wrote of the nature of man, and I feel it's a great example how man's behavior really hasn't changed, even with the technology and advancements in our century. Solomon said, "There was nothing new under the sun."

> The thing that hath been, it is that which shall be; and that which is done is that which shall be done: and there is no new thing under the sun. Is there any thing whereof it may be said, See, this is new? it hath been already of old time, which was before us. And I gave my heart to seek and search out by wisdom concerning all things that are done under heaven: this sore travail hath God given to the sons of man to be exercised therewith. I have seen all the works that are done under the sun; and, behold, all is vanity and vexation of spirit. (Eccl. 1:9–10, 13–14)

Read that whole book, even though some consider it depressing. Understand why Solomon wrote it. In this view, man without Christ is nothing, and has nothing to gain.

Peter covers more on this: "By which also he went and preached unto the spirits in prison; Which sometime were disobedient, when once the longsuffering of God waited in the days of Noah, while the ark was a preparing, wherein few, that is, eight souls were saved by water" (1 Pet. 3:19–20)

This shows us the people were obedient at one time, though at other times they were not.

Does this sound familiar? Yes, and praise God for Jesus in our lives. Because we are all sometimes disobedient to his written Word.

The only souls saved were in the ark as it was lifted up by the waves of the flood. All the other souls were destroyed by water, as they drowned.

The word saved (*diasōzō*) means to preserve through danger, to bring safely through to save, i.e. cure one who is sick, bring him through to save, keep from perishing, to save out of danger, escape and rescue.

A few references for this same word will help us to understand: Acts 28:4; 27:44; Luke 7:3.

Sinful behavior and lack of respect toward God's ways, like liberalism and unrestrained sexual behaviors, over time, corrupted the whole earth. How similar to the world in which we live in today. People would turn to quick remedies that would offer peace for a while: either drugs, strange false religious enchantments, or addictions (depending upon the desires, which a person pursued). Even though there may be a form of godliness, in reality, many deny the power of God by their behavior and actions.

> This know also, that in the last days perilous (hard, difficult) times shall come. For men shall be lovers of their own selves, covetous, boasters, proud, blasphemers, disobedient (not persuaded) to parents, unthankful, unholy, Without natural affection (hard-hearted towards kindred: — without natural affection), trucebreakers, false accusers, incontinent (without self-control, intemperate), fierce (not tame, savage, fierce), despisers of those that are good, Traitors, heady, highminded, lovers of pleasures more than lovers of God; Having a form (appearance) of godliness, but denying the power thereof: from such turn away. (2 Tim. 3:1–5)

Paul wrote this to Timothy since they considered that they were in the last times. Yet, when we read Paul's and Peter's letters, one would swear that it relates to us today.

Read what Paul said to Timothy, which was given to the church. Then see what you think. Read the whole chapter.

EATING AND DRINKING

The scriptures tell us they were eating and drinking. This may seem innocent but there is much more involved.

Gluttony (Latin: *gula*, derived from the Latin *gluttire*, meaning "to gulp down or swallow") means over-indulgence and over-consumption of food, drink, or wealth items, particularly as status symbols.

These temptations can destroy families, cultures, and your life.

"For as in the days that were before the flood they were eating and drinking, marrying and giving in marriage, until the day that Noe entered into the ark" (Matt. 24:38).

This is very interesting. Matthew must have read Genesis from the Torah, and Jesus put it all together through the Holy Ghost. It was revealed to Matthew; also, it was revealed by Luke in Luke 17:27.

The people were eating and drinking; they had plenty. They were not thankful nor giving glory to God. They treated it like any other day, not observing what was going on around them, staying in ignorance.

Does this seem like a good reason to destroy them, just for that action? It was more than this, the wickedness was spreading like a wildfire; *every reasoning in their thoughts was evil* in the way that God viewed it on the earth.

Why did the Holy Ghost have Matthew and Luke write this? To warn them, as well as those who would read it later.

We should always read and compare the references in God's Word.

As we read this, it seemed like a normal day of activities, and nothing was unusual. People were feasting or just having meals at home. We know from Genesis that the world had one language, one people. Yet the people were not seeking out the wisdom of God according to Noah's words and his actions. They were relaxed, enjoying life and their family, business, lifestyles, and the works of their hands. They were a prideful people.

Remember what the Lord said about pride (Prov. 6:16–19). I like to add this: "For if a man think himself to be something, when he is nothing, he deceiveth himself" (Gal. 6:3).

They were not paying attention or concerned with the times they were living in. God saw their wickedness beyond what we would think, but we can have a rather good idea by what we see today, and as we discussed earlier.

The Bible tells us that we should be satisfied with what we have. At times, we eat more than we should. Over time, we gain weight, and have other health issues because of it. We need to use wisdom and self-control. We are bringing these health problems upon ourselves over time. The Bible shows us this behavior all throughout God's Word. On eating too much and drinking: "Hear thou, my son, and be wise, and guide thine heart in the way. Be not among winebibbers; among riotous eaters of flesh: For the drunkard and the glutton shall come to poverty: and drowsiness shall clothe a man with rags" (Prov. 23:19–21)

This warns us to use wisdom. Do not join with those who drink too much wine or gorge themselves on food, for drunkards and gluttons become poor, and their clothes become rags. *They bring this on themselves:*

> When thou sittest to eat with a ruler, consider diligently what is before thee: And put a knife to thy throat, if thou be a man given to appetite. Be not desirous of his dainties: for they are deceitful meat. Labour not to be rich: cease from thine own wisdom. Wilt thou set thine eyes upon that which is not? for riches certainly make themselves wings; they fly away as an eagle toward heaven. Eat thou not the bread of him that hath an evil eye, neither desire thou his dainty meats: For as he thinketh in

his heart, so is he: Eat and drink, saith he to thee; but his heart is not with thee. The morsel which thou hast eaten shalt thou vomit up, and lose thy sweet words. (Prov. 23:1–8)

Our physical appetite shows our ability to control ourselves. If we are unable to control our eating habits, we are probably also unable to control other problems, habits, and addictions.

We may consider our thoughts on lust, covetousness, anger, and being unable to keep our mouth from gossip, accusations, or strife. We need to bring our thoughts into subjection to God's Word, and the Holy Ghost gives us strength to assist us in this action. Do not allow the desire for food to control us. We are to discipline our appetites by seeking God's advice, and seeking out help from the scriptures through the spirit.

Look at the next scripture that gives a strong indication of this wickedness:

This know also, that in the last days perilous(hard, difficult) times shall come. For men shall be lovers of their own selves, covetous, boasters, proud, blasphemers, disobedient to parents, unthankful, unholy, Without natural affection, trucebreakers, false accusers, incontinent (without self-control), fierce, despisers of those that are good, Traitors, heady, highminded, lovers of pleasures more than lovers of God. (2 Tim. 3:1–4)

God gives the answer on what to do:

(For the weapons of our warfare are not carnal, but mighty through God to the pulling down of strong holds); Casting down imaginations (reasoning), and every high thing that exalteth itself against the knowledge of God, and bringing into captivity every thought to the obedience of Christ; And having in a readiness to revenge all disobedience, when your obedience is fulfilled. (2 Cor. 10:4–6)

Take those thoughts and replace them with God's written Word.

Peter has more to say on this:

Simon Peter, a servant and an apostle of Jesus Christ, to them that have obtained like precious faith with us through the righteousness of God and our Saviour Jesus Christ: Grace and peace be multiplied unto you through the knowledge of God, and of Jesus our Lord, According as his divine power hath given unto us all things that pertain unto life and godliness, through the knowledge of him that hath called (invited) us to glory and virtue: Whereby are given unto us exceeding great and precious promises: that by these ye might be partakers of the divine nature, having escaped the corruption that is in the world through lust. And beside this, giving all diligence, add to your faith virtue; and to virtue knowledge; And to knowledge temperance (self-control); and to temperance patience (endurance); and to patience godliness; And to godliness brotherly kindness; and to brotherly kindness charity. For if these things be in you, and abound (to make more), they make you that ye shall neither be barren nor unfruitful in the knowledge of our Lord Jesus Christ. (2 Pet. 1:1–8)

These scriptures help us to understand who we are and what we have in Christ. We can see *that our war is over* because of Christ and his resurrection. We can rest and have peace by submitting ourselves to this truth. *We still have battles*, but we can have the victory as we grow and learn from Jesus Christ. We are free, and can walk free in his spirit resisting these temptations. Resisting temptation is one of the battles that we all face each day.

We have the ability to say "no" to anything that does not agree with God's Word. We have a free will, and should not be ruled over. We can take that stand. We have to make that decision, and God will help us as we work together with him.

The fruit of the spirit is provided freely to all believers. Yet we can increase it, by studying and reading God's written Word, and can experience the fruit of the spirit as we go through temptations and tribulations in this world.

> But the fruit of the Spirit is love, joy, peace, long-suffering (patience) gentleness, goodness, faith, Meekness, temperance (self-control): against such there is no law. And they that are Christ's have crucified the flesh with the affections and lusts. If we live in the Spirit, let us also walk in the Spirit. Let us not be desirous of vain glory, provoking one another, envying one another. (Gal. 5:22–26)

According to Matthew 24:38, people did not see what was really happening to them in their culture and the times they were facing. They heard rumors off and on about Noah building this crazy ark. It didn't make sense since it had never rained and the ark wasn't on any sea at that time. They didn't give heed and it cost them everything. *They ignored the signs of the times.*

Drinking was a problem too. It would cause a man to stumble in judgment or discernment.

Look at this example in the book of Isaiah:

> But they also have erred through wine, and through strong drink are out of the way; the priest and the prophet have erred through strong drink, they are swallowed up of wine, they are out of

the way through strong drink; they err in vision, they stumble in judgment. For all tables are full of vomit and filthiness, so that there is no place clean. (Isa. 28:7–8)

God used drinking to show their spiritual condition. Here is another example of drinking:

And when the people saw that Moses delayed to come down out of the mount, the people gathered themselves together unto Aaron, and said unto him, Up, make us gods, which shall go before us; for as for this Moses, the man that brought us up out of the land of Egypt, we wot not what is become of him. And Aaron said unto them, Break off the golden earrings, which are in the ears of your wives, of your sons, and of your daughters, and bring them unto me. And all the people brake off the golden earrings which were in their ears, and brought them unto Aaron. And he received them at their hand, and fashioned it with a graving tool, after he had made it a molten calf: and they said, These be thy gods, O Israel, which brought thee up out of the land of Egypt. And when Aaron saw it, he built an altar before it; and Aaron made proclamation, and said, "Tomorrow is a feast to the Lord." And they rose up early on the morrow, and offered burnt offerings, and brought peace offerings; and the people sat down to eat and to drink, and rose up to play. And the Lord said unto Moses, "Go, get thee down; for thy people, which thou broughtest out of the land of Egypt, have corrupted themselves." (Exod. 32:1–7)

Matthew 24:38 alone shows the times that Jesus warned about.

As we read this chapter, keep in mind to whom it was first written and why. Matthew was written before 70 AD and concerns the times when Jesus was here, which was before his death and resurrection. It was still the Old Testament times, and Jesus was speaking about his people, Israel, the Jewish nation under Roman occupation.

To fully understand Matthew 24, along with other books in the New Testament that give these references, you must read and understand Daniel, as Jesus said in Matthew 24:15.

Jesus wanted them to know about the coming destruction to the temple and buildings, that false prophets were coming to bring peace (deceptive world peace), and the gathering of the saints (the church meeting the Lord in the air at the resurrection, which today is referenced as the Rapture).

The seven-year tribulation and the second coming of Christ (with his wrath), plus many other events are written by John in the book of Revelation. That is just the start of the principles and precepts one would have to cover.

There are many views in the churches just on these subjects alone. Additionally, more books would need to be referenced on these subjects of study. Nevertheless, God uses his body (all of us) with what we know to work with each other. Yet, sadly, prejudice, pride, traditions, erred doctrines, and weak translations hinder us.

John wrote of the behavior to not love the world or behave like it:

Love not the world, neither the things that are in the world. If any man love the world, the love of the Father is not in him. For all that is in the world, the lust of the flesh, and the lust of the eyes, and the pride of life, is not of the Father, but is of the world. And the world passeth away, and the lust thereof: but he that doeth the will of God abideth for ever. (1 John 2:15–17)

As we read Matthew 24:38, we can see they were feasting, marrying, and giving into marriage, showing their attention was not on the ark that Noah was building *as a warning sign.*

They had a world of prosperity, world unity, unaccepted sexual behavior, technology, knowledge of science, and praising the works of their own hands. We have no idea of their advancements.

The rain came, and the earth was broken up from beneath to destroy them all and everything they had. Are those days coming upon us?

Many agree that the signs are all around us.

Yet, could there be a sign that has happened to show the times we are living in?

THE FIG TREE

We know that when Israel became a nation, it was not just by chance or because the idea was popular in the United Nations. This event was disputed by Jewish rabbi leaders who said, "Only the Messiah would be the one who would reestablish Israel and open the eastern gate." Yet when the homeland was opened, some then thought differently.

Most rabbis thought otherwise. Their enemies wanted it to cease. On Israel's Independence Day, Israel had war with the surrounding nations that came against them. Countless testimonies said "the God of Israel" surely had visited his land once again.

After the war of 1948, Israel became a nation and a state among the Arab states. Then came the 1956 war in which Israel occupied the Sinai. In 1967, Israel took Jerusalem and all of the Temple mount and surroundings.

Later Israel gave some land back (which were parts of the Temple mount locations) to have peace. They returned the Sinai because it was not a part of the land of Israel, but it belonged to Esau. They did this either knowingly because of scripture, or unknowingly.

They returned the Sinai in order to have peace with Egypt, at least this was the accepted explanation that was given.

Then in 1973, the Yom Kippur War was an attack from Syria. In 1982, the Lebanese War was fought in the southern part of Lebanon, which Israel occupied for a while; over the years, the conflict would restart again in 2005, 2008, even to this day.

It is very interesting from scripture that the Lord spoke to Moses and told Joshua that they should take the land little by little.

"And the Lord thy God will put out those nations before thee by little and little: thou mayest not consume them at once, lest the beasts of the field increase upon thee" (Deut. 7:22).

(Note: Read chapters 1–7 to get the full picture. This is at the end of Moses' forty years of wandering in the wilderness when he took the land on the eastern side of the Jordan River. Then after Moses died, Joshua took the western side.)

Could this be the same pattern that Israel is facing today, *taking the land little by little?* We will see.

Israel wants peace, and that is clear. Notice that certain locations must be secured in order for Israel to have that peace with her enemies. It's when she is forced into another major war that more land is occupied and taken. If you read the book of Joshua, it was the same way. Joshua took land little by little.

One must note that it is God's (Yahweh's) land. He doesn't do this because he thinks that they are *more righteous than other people.*

Look at what he said in Deuteronomy 9:4–6:

Speak not thou in thine heart, after that the Lord thy God hath cast them out from before thee, saying, For my righteousness the Lord hath brought me in to possess this land: but for the wickedness of these nations the Lord doth drive them out from before thee. Not for thy righteousness, or for the uprightness of thine heart, dost thou go to possess their land: but for the wickedness of these nations the Lord thy God doth drive them out from before thee, and that he may perform the word which the Lord sware unto thy fathers, Abraham, Isaac, and Jacob. Understand therefore, that the Lord thy God giveth thee not this good land to possess it for thy righteousness; for thou art a stiff necked people. (Deut. 9:4–6)

God allowed Joshua to take all of the land because of the promise he made to Abraham, Isaac, and Jacob (Israel). Joshua and Caleb wanted to take the land forty years earlier and the others rebelled. We read that Joshua did not take *all of the land* because he wanted peace. This cost him later because of other wars.

Consider what Numbers 33:55 says: "But if ye will not drive out the inhabitants of the land from before you; then it shall come to pass, that those which ye let remain of them shall be pricks in your eyes, and thorns in your sides, and shall vex you in the land wherein ye dwell."

Joshua went as far as Hamath, and ceased his attack. He never went beyond that to the Euphrates River. They fought near there and had battles, yet never took those locations. Up to the *Euphrates River is the full promise* of the land of Israel spoken to Abram in Genesis 15:18–21, which will come *in Christ's reign for one thousand years*.

God used Joshua's actions to draw our attention to the prophet Jeremiah (and to what he would proclaim in Jeremiah 30). Israel would return to the land that *their fathers possessed.* This is a good point to consider and to look for in scripture.

The Land of Abraham extended from the Egyptian River to the Euphrates River. This land would come into possession after the seven-year tribulation when Christ would reign physically for one thousand years on Earth with the believers.

This was that promise that God made to Abraham and to all his people.

The land that Moses and Joshua took possession of was from the *Egyptian River up to Hamath.*

Is this the land that Jeremiah spoke about that Israel would take in the last days?

A few references to look over: Jeremiah 16:15, 30:3–4. (Note: it speaks of the land that their fathers possessed.)

Who were their fathers that possessed the land and how much land did they occupy?

It wasn't Abraham, because the Lord told him he was in a land that was not his, but that this land would be given to his seed (Gen. 12:1–2, 7, 15:13).

The fathers are Moses and Joshua. We can understand from scripture which land they took, and then believe God at his word. We can share with others what the Lord is going to do, so that when it happens they might believe and come to the Messiah, which is Jesus our Lord.

This is not to convince or to convert anyone. Only the Lord convicts the hearts through the Holy Spirit, and it takes time to study this further. This is to provoke one's thoughts, and to consider this for study.

If you know these things, praise the Lord, and if not, praise the Lord that you're going on a journey in scripture that will bless you and amaze you. God (Yahweh) of Israel is moving, and his salvation, Jesus, "Yeshua", is the only way to the father.

"Neither is there salvation in any other: for there is none other name under heaven given among men, whereby we must be saved" (Acts 4:12).

There is another point that should be addressed. Daniel's prophecy is sealed *until the time of the end* (Dan. 12:4). The word "time" in Hebrew is "fixed time or season or event" and is a period of time.

There are interesting points that the angel Gabriel reveals about the truth of Daniel's people, the seventy weeks, Jerusalem, and the land to which they shall return in the last days.

I hope this quickens your spirit and enhances your love for God's written Word so you will study it with diligence.

Jesus used physical manifestations to explain his teachings. The fig tree is known because of these scriptures:

"I found Israel like grapes in the wilderness; I saw your fathers as the firstripe in the fig tree at her first time: but they went to Baalpeor, and separated themselves unto that shame; and their abominations were according as they loved" (Hosea 9:10).

"Now in the morning as he returned into the city, he hungered. And when he saw a fig tree in the way, he came to it, and found nothing thereon, but leaves only, and said unto it, Let no fruit grow on thee henceforward for ever. And presently the fig tree withered away" (Matt. 21:18–19).

"He spake also this parable; A certain man had a fig tree planted in his vineyard; and he came and sought fruit thereon, and found none" (Luke 13:6).

"He hath laid my vine waste, and barked my fig tree: he hath made it clean bare, and cast it away; the branches thereof are made white" (Joel 1:7).

Now learn a parable of the fig tree; When his branch is yet tender, and putteth forth leaves, ye know that summer is nigh: So likewise ye, when ye shall see all these things, know that it is near, even at the doors. Verily I say unto you, "This generation shall not pass, till all these things be fulfilled. Heaven and earth shall pass away, but my words shall not pass away. But of that day and hour knoweth no man, no, not the angels of heaven, but my Father only. But as the days of Noah were, so shall also the coming of the Son of man be. For as in the days that were before the flood they were eating and drinking, marrying and giving in marriage, until the day that Noe entered into the ark, And knew not until the flood came, and took them all away; so shall also the coming of the Son of man be. Then shall two be in the field; the one shall be taken, and the other left. Two women shall be grinding at the mill; the one shall be taken, and the other left. Watch therefore: for ye know not what hour your Lord doth come. But know this, that if the goodman of the house had known in what watch the thief would come, he would have watched, and would not have suffered his house to be broken up. Therefore be ye also ready: for in such an hour as ye think not the Son of man cometh." (Matt. 24:32–44)

Many have different views on this: the fig tree and all these verses, yet, the days of Noah are in context.

If we are living in these days, we are going to see some amazing things, and we will not just be telling people Jesus is coming, but showing them, just as in the days of Noah.

SODOM AND GOMORRAH AND THE DAYS OF LOT

—◆◆◆—

When we read this, we think right away, *God placed his wrath on the city because of different sexual interactions*. The word "Sodom" in Hebrew is *Cĕdom*, "burning." A Canaanite city, usually paired with Gomorrah, located in the area of the Dead Sea and the Jordan River; both cities destroyed by God in judgment.

We think it's because of their lifestyles, and wicked culture that they were destroyed.

Yet, it's far worse than we first thought.

It is more familiar than we ever imagined.

Could this be related to the days we are living in, compared to the days before the flood in many ways?

We will see why God decided that he had enough, and took them away.

We will also read what the prophet Ezekiel wrote first of the sins and wickedness of Jerusalem.

Next, we will read a few verses and point out a few things.

"And thine elder sister is Samaria, she and her daughters that dwell at thy left hand: and thy younger sister, that dwelleth at thy right hand, is Sodom and her daughters" (Ezek. 16:46).

When you read the chapter, you will see that it is talking about Jerusalem, other cities, and their sins.

"Again the word of the Lord came unto me, saying, 'Son of man, cause Jerusalem to know her abominations'" (Ezek. 16:1–2).

> Yet hast thou not walked after their ways, nor done after their abominations: but, as if that were a very little thing, thou wast corrupted more than they in all thy ways.
>
> (*It tells us Jerusalem was more corrupt.*)
>
> "As I live," saith the Lord God, "Sodom thy sister hath not done, she nor her daughters, as thou hast done, thou and thy daughters. Behold, this was the iniquity of thy sister Sodom, pride, fulness of bread, and abundance of idleness was in her and in her daughters, neither did she strengthen the hand of the poor and needy. And they were haughty, and committed abomination before me: therefore I took them away as I saw good. Neither hath Samaria committed half of thy sins; but thou hast multiplied thine abominations more than they, and hast justified thy sisters in all thine abominations which thou hast done. Thou also, which hast judged thy sisters, bear thine own shame for thy sins that thou hast committed more abominable than they: they are more righteous than thou: yea, be thou confounded also, and bear thy shame, in that thou hast justified thy sisters." (Ezek. 16:47–52)

God warned Israel, namely Jerusalem that they committed more abominations and sins than those other cities. They had judged their other sisters (cities), in their pride.

What is interesting is that God lays out the sins they committed.

In Ezekiel 16:49, it is written: "Behold, this was the iniquity of thy sister Sodom, pride, fulness of bread, and abundance of idleness was in her and in her daughters, neither did she strengthen the hand of the poor and needy." We will compare this with what we went over.

THE SINS OF SODOM

1. First thing spoken of is pride.

God hates pride and Lucifer fell because of rejection and pride. It spread to Eve, Adam, Cain, and his descendants as well as Seth's (Adam's third son) and his descendants.

Pride comes up in many ways. Our appearance, position, accomplishments, and wealth. *A self-love.* This is the message Satan was teaching. If we do a word search on pride in a Bible concordance, we will find out many things.

Start in Proverbs and Psalms for word searches on "pride", and see what the Lord thinks.

2. Next, they had plenty to eat. Prosperity and peace all around them. When a person has much, they might forget God, and trust in themselves, they also can become un-thankful and take things for granted.

3. They had idleness. They had too much time on their hand, which got them into trouble with temptation.

There were no written scriptures at that time. The Torah (the five books of the Law) was written by Moses, though he might have been assisted by a scribe.

Yet, in Noah's days, they could have listened to those who knew God and respected his ways, and did what God commanded.

4. They didn't assist the poor. They did not help those in need by mercy and grace. They needed to have compassion to help the poor, so in return when they are able, they could do likewise to help others in need.

5. Committed abominations before me. God speaks of sins in the Bible, but when he speaks of abominations, it is far worse in his eyes. From worshipping other gods, the host of heaven (zodiac), improper sexual behavior, and raising their hand against the good and innocent.

These were like *the days of Noah,* and the people corrupted themselves.

Looking up this word "idleness" we can find:

Idleness: the quality, state, or condition of being lazy, inactive.

A person who is idle doesn't have a goal, commitment, or desire to improve.

This isn't just being related to work, but to improve our behavior, spiritual life, and physical body and mind.

Yet, they were destroyed because they didn't submit to God's warnings and judgments.

The poor and needy is the next point.

God did not like it that they forgot the poor and those in need. We should help those if it's in our power to do so. *We should never despise the poor.*

My brethren, have not the faith (steadfastness) of our Lord Jesus Christ, the Lord of glory, with respect of persons. For if there come unto your assembly a man with a gold ring, in goodly apparel, and there come in also a poor man in vile raiment; and ye have respect to him that weareth the gay clothing, and say unto him, "Sit thou here in a good place; and say to the poor, 'Stand thou there, or sit here under my footstool:' are ye not then partial in yourselves, and are become judges of evil thoughts? Hearken, my beloved brethren, Hath not God chosen the poor of this world rich in faith, and heirs of the kingdom which he hath promised to them that love him? But ye have despised the poor. Do not rich men oppress you, and draw you before the judgment seats? Do not they blaspheme that worthy name by the which ye are called? If ye fulfil the royal law according to the scripture, Thou shalt love thy neighbour as thyself, ye do well: But if ye have respect to persons, ye commit sin, and are convinced of the law as transgressors." (James 2:1–9)

"If there be among you a poor man of one of thy brethren within any of thy gates in thy land which the Lord thy God giveth thee, thou shalt not harden thine heart, nor shut thine hand from thy poor brother" (Deut. 15:7).

The Bible also says not to allow others to place their trust in you alone and to *take advantage of your generosity*.

"Surety", in Hebrew, *ârab*, aw-rab, means to pledge, exchange, mortgage, engage, occupy, undertake for, give pledges, be or become surety, take on pledge, give in pledge.

They need to seek after the Lord after they have gracefully benefited those who helped them.

"He that is surety for a stranger shall smart for it: and he that hateth suretiship is sure" (Prov. 11:15)

My son, if thou be surety for thy friend, if thou hast stricken thy hand with a stranger, Thou art snared with the words of thy mouth, thou art taken with the words of thy mouth. Do this now, my son, and deliver thyself, when thou art come into the hand of thy friend; go, humble thyself, and make sure thy friend. Give not sleep to thine eyes, nor slumber to thine eyelids. Deliver thyself as a roe from the hand of the hunter, and as a bird from the hand of the fowler. (Prov. 6:1–5)

"Be not thou one of them that strike hands, or of them that are sureties for debts" (Prov. 22:26).

It seems that Sodom and the other cities forgot their poor and lifted up themselves with pride. We must be careful not to behave this way.

God saw how these people were behaving by their actions in not reaching out to others.

"And they were haughty, and committed abomination before me: therefore I took them away as I saw good" (Ezek. 16:50).

Could this be the recipe for disaster? For a city or nation? Yes, and God has a reservation for *all nations* at an appointed time he has set.

"'For I am with thee,' saith the Lord, 'to save thee: though I make a full end of all nations whither I have scattered thee, yet I will not make a full end of thee: but I will correct thee in measure, and will not leave thee altogether unpunished'" (Jer. 30:11).

God destroyed the world with a flood of water; he will not do that again.

Next time it will be a *flood of fire and destruction*. This is known as "The Wrath of God", which the prophets wrote about and which is at the *end of the great tribulation*.

THE DAYS OF LOT

Lot and his family were running for their lives as the angels of the Lord said, "We can't do anything until we get you out."

The angels grabbed them and pulled Lot and his wife and his two daughters quickly out of the city. Their family's possessions, friends, and other family members were left behind, as they ran.

They passed markets, places where food was served, and locations where business transactions were conducted. Discussions in politics, and common every day disputes, were heard.

They passed homes of the rich and powerful, and of the poor. There was enjoyment, laughter, and pleasure. In other areas, abominations that should not be spoken.

As they fled from the city, they were told not to look back when the destruction would come once out of the region of the valley.

There are many things we can learn from this.

We will start with Abram and Lot's situation among them with their people:

> And Abram said unto Lot, "Let there be no strife, I pray thee, between me and thee, and between my herdmen and thy herdmen; for we be brethren. Is not the whole land before thee? separate thyself, I pray thee, from me: if thou wilt take the left hand, then I will go to the right; or if thou depart to the right hand, then I will go to the left." And Lot lifted up his eyes, and beheld all the plain of Jordan, that it was well watered every where, before the Lord destroyed Sodom and Gomorrah, even as the garden of the Lord, like the land of Egypt, as thou comest unto Zoar. Then Lot chose him all the plain of Jordan; and Lot journeyed east: and they separated themselves the one from the other. Abram dwelled in the land of Canaan, and Lot dwelled in the cities of the plain, and pitched his tent toward Sodom. But the men of Sodom were wicked and sinners before the Lord exceedingly. (Gen. 13:8–13)

A quick thought: Sodom and Gomorrah were even as the Garden of the Lord? Like the land of Egypt? What we see today in that region is not as it was back then. They were some beautiful places, but sin, the curse, and wickedness destroyed them.

Let's continue: Abram gave Lot a choice, and Lot set his tents toward Sodom and the cities of the plain. At first,

Lot just set his tents toward that way, but eventually they were in the city itself.

We can see he made the wrong choice, as this influence would change his people and those he loved forever.

As you continue to read these chapters, there were many other events, wars, and the promise that God made with Abraham about his seed and the Promised Land.

Then, as we continue to read, three men appeared to Abraham, and spoke to him about having a son as recorded in Genesis chapter 18. These men were angels from the Lord.

Now notice this:

> And the Lord said, "Shall I hide from Abraham that thing which I do; seeing that Abraham shall surely become a great and mighty nation, and all the nations of the earth shall be blessed in him? For I know him, that he will command his children and his household after him, and they shall keep the way of the Lord, to do justice and judgment; that the Lord may bring upon Abraham that which he hath spoken of him." And the Lord said, "Because the cry of Sodom and Gomorrah is great, and because their sin is very grievous; I will go down now, and see whether they have done altogether according to the cry of it, which is come unto me; and if not, I will know." And the men turned their faces from thence, and went toward Sodom: but Abraham stood yet before the Lord. And Abraham drew near, and said, "Wilt thou also destroy the righteous with the wicked?" (Gen. 18:17–23)

Notice what happened next:

Abraham said:

> Peradventure (Hebrew: Perhaps) there be fifty righteous within the city: wilt thou also destroy

and not spare the place for the fifty righteous that are therein? That be far from thee to do after this manner, to slay the righteous with the wicked: and that the righteous should be as the wicked, that be far from thee: Shall not the Judge of all the earth do right? And the Lord said, "If I find in Sodom fifty righteous within the city, then I will spare all the place for their sakes." And Abraham answered and said, "Behold now, I have taken upon me to speak unto the Lord, which am but dust and ashes: Peradventure there shall lack five of the fifty righteous: wilt thou destroy all the city for lack of five? And he said, If I find there forty and five, I will not destroy it." And he spake unto him yet again, and said, "Peradventure there shall be forty found there. And he said, I will not do it for forty's sake." And he said unto him, "Oh let not the Lord be angry, and I will speak: Peradventure there shall thirty be found there." And he said, "I will not do it, if I find thirty there." And he said, "Behold now, I have taken upon me to speak unto the Lord: Peradventure there shall be twenty found there." And he said, "I will not destroy it for twenty's sake." And he said, "Oh let not the Lord be angry, and I will speak yet but this once: Peradventure ten shall be found there." And he said, "I will not destroy it for ten's sake." And the Lord went his way, as soon as he had left communing with Abraham: and Abraham returned unto his place. (Gen. 18:24–33)

Why did Abraham try to get the amount lowered? Because he knew God's mercy, and he had a plan.

Abraham knew Lot was righteous, his wife, and most likely his two daughters, and their husbands (Gen. 19:12). This would amount to six people, not to forget the parents from both husbands, which would come to ten people, if they were alive.

Yet we know the story. Lot, his wife, and two daughters were practically dragged out by the angels of the Lord. This was only four righteous people.

Lot got himself into trouble hanging around these people, and it caused all of his own people to be drawn into this situation.

Look at this scripture:

> And turning the cities of Sodom and Gomorrah into ashes condemned them with an overthrow, making them an ensample unto those that after should live ungodly; And delivered just Lot, vexed with the filthy conversation of the wicked:
>
> (Just, means justified, because it was not just Lot who was delivered, it was his wife and two daughters who were removed out of the city. "Vex" means to wear out. Lot was worn out by their sins and wickedness.)
>
> For that righteous man dwelling among them, in seeing and hearing, vexed his righteous soul from day to day with their unlawful deeds; The Lord knoweth how to deliver the godly out of temptations, and to reserve the unjust unto the day of judgment to be punished. (2 Pet. 2:6–9)

God knows how to deliver the godly, and he sent his angels to save their lives. The unjust were destroyed in the destruction of those cities in which they lived.

Here are a few more scriptures about Lot from which we can learn:

> And as it was in the days of Noe, so shall it be also in the days of the Son of man. They did eat, they drank, they married wives, they were given in

marriage, until the day that Noah entered into the ark, and the flood came, and destroyed them all. Likewise also as it was in the days of Lot; they did eat, they drank, they bought, they sold, they planted, they builded; But the same day that Lot went out of Sodom it rained fire and brimstone from heaven, and destroyed them all. Even thus shall it be in the day when the Son of man is revealed. In that day, he which shall be upon the housetop, and his stuff in the house, let him not come down to take it away: and he that is in the field, let him likewise not return back. Remember Lot's wife. Whosoever shall seek to save his life shall lose it; and whosoever shall lose his life shall preserve it. (Luke 17:26–33)

God will save his own, but the wicked, those without Christ, shall face that wrath when Christ is revealed to the world after the tribulation (Matt. 24:29–30).

I'm not talking about our gathering together to him to meet Him in the clouds (1 Thess. 4:17). Rather I'm referring to the wrath when Christ comes to destroy those nations that come against Israel at the end of the Great Tribulation.

The Rapture event begins years before this event. When the dead in Christ rise first, and we are changed (our bodies) in a twinkling of an eye, and meet him in the air (1 Cor. 15:51–58; 1 Thess. 5:1–4, 9; 2 Thess. 2:1–3).

Millions of Christians call this event the Rapture.

"Rapture" is an English noun derived from the Latin verb *rapiō*, with a literal meaning of "caught up" or "to snatch away."

This starts in a time of peace (deceptive peace) and safety according to Paul, John, and Jeremiah, to name just a few servants of God that wrote about the false peace that was coming.

After a major war (because of land disputes in Israel with those who fight against Israel) according to Bible prophecy, then a false peace will be established.

Some take God's written Word literally, every word. Some take it symbolically. Others take it both symbolically and literally, depending on the context, precepts, and on what Jesus said, or on events compared with other scriptures.

Others take it by revelation of the spirit, depending from which denominational or nondenominational church they have been taught.

There are many views among Christians regarding Christ's return (including whether it will occur in one event or two events), and various views regarding the destination of our gathering to meet him in the air, described in 1 Thessalonians 4:13–17, and 2 Thessalonians 2:1–2.

This book will not cover this in detail, but I do have studies that can be provided, if you join us on Facebook, or my author's Facebook site. If requested, we will provide them.

What this book is trying to share is whether the times of old will be repeated, whether there will be warnings similar to back then. We need to see what Jesus said that we might be able to escape this time of trouble coming.

Keep in mind, Lot's family suffered hardships, especially his wife when she looked back.

Noah's family was saved, because they were in the ark. *These subjects are two different things to think about.*

The days of Noah reveal the protection they have in the ark, just as we are protected and sealed by his spirit to be saved. Jesus as an example of our Ark of protection that we are in him by faith, having peace and rest.

The days of Lot refers to those who will have to flee, and to those who will be destroyed when they are left behind in the Great Tribulation. These are two different points that should be studied, of which Jesus, Paul, John, Daniel, and others wrote.

We will now return back to where we were.

"Even as Sodom and Gomorrah, and the cities about them in like manner, giving themselves over to fornication, and going after strange flesh, are set forth for an example, suffering the vengeance of eternal fire" (Jude 1:7).

The people of the city practiced many types of fornication and wickedness, and the Bible warns of what we bring upon ourselves if we reject the natural use of women and men. There were other abominations that were practiced as you read God's Word. God loves people, and he knows what evil they bring on themselves. Satan enhances it. Satan is the destroyer, not God. God does use his angels when needed according to scripture to accomplish his will.

Consider this warning in Leviticus:

Thou shalt not lie with mankind, as with womankind: it is abomination. Neither shalt thou lie with any beast to defile thyself therewith: neither shall any woman stand before a beast to lie down thereto: it is confusion. Defile not ye yourselves in any of these things: for in all these the nations are defiled which I cast out before you: And the land is defiled: therefore I do visit the iniquity thereof upon it, and the land itself vomiteth out her inhabitants. (Lev. 18:22–25)

God cast those out of the land of Israel that did these things, to give Israeli people the land of Israel.

Can we say this type of behavior existed before the flood of Noah and after? Yes, and it will get worse.

Look at the book of Revelation: "For all nations have drunk of the wine of the wrath of her fornication, and the kings of the earth have committed fornication with her, and the merchants of the earth are waxed rich through the abundance of her delicacies" (Rev. 18:3).

Think about this and compare it with the sins of Sodom in Ezekiel 16:46–52.

Lot was vexed (2 Pet. 2:7) when he joined himself to that city.

"Vex" means to wear out; *kataponeō*, to tire down with toil, exhaust with labor, to afflict or oppress with evils, to make trouble for, to treat roughly.

Because of Lot's fellowship with others, he brought problems to his family and friends that we cannot imagine.

He lost everything, even his wife.

What can we learn from this? Just as Jesus taught and spoke of this himself, as did his servants: if we love the sins of the world, we will be vexed by it, just as Lot was.

This also shows me that God loves us, but he will not put up with wickedness and rebellion. We can invite hardship and death at an early age.

God knows how this evil will spread, deceive, weaken, harm, and destroy.

These warnings of Noah and Lot should make us welcome each day and be thankful, and seek after his grace as we study and read from his Holy Word.

These scriptures or accounts should not upset us, but should encourage us to be examples of Jesus, not of the world. To love others just as God has loved us:

> Jesus said unto him, "Thou shalt love the Lord thy God with all thy heart, and with all thy soul, and with all thy mind. This is the first and great commandment. And the second is like unto it, 'Thou shalt love thy neighbour as thyself.' On these two commandments hang all the law and the prophets." (Matt. 22:37–40)

We love the person, as we speak the truth, not the behavior.

The Ark

In Me You Might Have Peace

At that day ye shall ask in my name: and I say not unto you, that I will pray the Father for you: For the Father himself loveth you, because ye have loved me, and have believed that I came out from God. I came forth from the Father, and am come into the world: again, I leave the world, and go to the Father. His disciples said unto him, "Lo, now speakest thou plainly, and speakest no proverb. Now are we sure that thou knowest all things, and needest not that any man should ask thee: by this we believe that thou camest forth from God." Jesus answered them, "Do ye now believe? Behold, the hour cometh, yea, is now come, that ye shall be scattered, every man to his own, and shall leave me alone: and yet I am not alone, because the Father is with me. These things I have spoken unto you, that in me ye might have peace. In the world ye shall have tribulation: but be of good cheer; I have overcome the world." (John 16:26–33)

The night before his crucifixion, Jesus was with his disciples speaking to them, for the time would come soon that he would be taken, killed, and then raised the third day.

Jesus spoke many times over the years in parables and mysteries about his death.

Please read John chapters 14–17 to get the fullness.

Jesus was speaking of what was coming, yet he was careful not to give details of the redemption. What was the reason that he didn't explain it in detail?

Paul spoke of this:

That your faith should not stand in the wisdom of men, but in the power of God. Howbeit we speak wisdom among them that are perfect: yet not the wisdom of this world, nor of the princes of this world, that come to nought: But we speak the wisdom of God in a mystery (secret mystery) even the hidden wisdom, which God ordained before the world unto our glory: Which none of the princes of this world knew: for had they known it, they would not have crucified the Lord of glory. (1 Cor. 2:5–8)

This is very important. We know that man's redemption was hidden from the devil and from men. If the princes of this world found out, *they would not have crucified our Lord and there would be no Resurrection.*

There would be no death on the cross, shedding of blood, burial, or Christ's spiritual soul going to Paradise (which was in the earth), and then into the heart of the earth, fulfilling the prophecy of Jonah: "For as Jonah was three days and three nights in the whale's belly; so shall the Son of man be three days and three nights in the heart of the earth" (Matt. 12:40).

The heart of the earth is the bottomless pit for the cursed without redemption. See my first book, *Beyond Paradise: The Story of Our Ultimate Redemption.*

If Christ had not died, there would be no salvation, new birth, or *the promises of the life now and yet to come* (1 Tim. 4:8).

If the enemy knew what Jesus' death would produce, they would not have crucified him. Praise God, it was hidden from them.

"But as it is written, Eye hath not seen, nor ear heard, neither have entered into the heart of man, the things which God hath prepared for them that love him. But God hath revealed them unto us by his Spirit: for the Spirit searcheth all things, yea, the deep things of God" (1 Cor. 2:9–10).

Our peace is in Jesus, even in trouble. Jesus is the one who reveals that true peace and rest.

He is our safety and confidence. Just as Noah and his family were safe in the ark which he built, we are safe from eternal destruction because we are in Jesus.

The ark of Noah was an example of what Jesus was coming to be. Jesus was also coming to bring us peace, safety, and rest within us in many ways, not just providing salvation to those who call on him, but also in our Christian walk to uphold that protection, if we believe.

IN HIM

Being "in him" gives understanding being saved, born again, "new creations" (of our spirit), because of Christ. Here is a list of scriptures that speak of being in him:

"For God so loved the world, that he gave his only begotten Son, that whosoever believeth in him should not perish, but have everlasting life." (John 3:16)

"For in him we live, and move, and have our being; as certain also of your own poets have said, For we are also his offspring." (Acts 17:28)

"For he hath made him to be sin for us, who knew no sin; that we might be made the righteousness of God in him." (2 Cor. 5:21)

"In whom we have redemption through his blood, the forgiveness of sins, according to the riches of his grace." (Eph. 1:7)

"In whom ye also trusted, after that ye heard the word of truth, the gospel of your salvation: in whom also after that ye believed, ye were sealed with that holy Spirit of promise." (Eph. 1:13)

"Since we heard of your faith in Christ Jesus, and of the love which ye have to all the saints." (Col. 1:4)

"For in him dwelleth all the fulness of the Godhead bodily. And ye are complete in him, which is the head of all principality and power." (Col. 2:9–10)

"Hereby know we that we dwell in him, and he in us, because he hath given us of his Spirit." (1 John 4:13)

"And this is the confidence that we have in him, that, if we ask any thing according to his will, he heareth us." (1 John 5:14)

There are many scriptures written about "in him." As you do a word-study, you will find more.

Here is a small list of scriptures you can add to your Bible:

Romans 3:24; 5:17; 8:1–2, 10, 39; 9:1; 12:5;
1 Corinthians 1:2; 15:22; 16:24
2 Corinthians 1:21; 2:14; 3:14; 5:19; 11:3
Galatians 2:16; 3:28
Ephesians 1:12
Colossians 1:4
2 Timothy 1:9; 2:1

Before we go any further, we will talk about this phrase "in him." The Greek word *en* means by, with, in place, and in, to give a few translations. It also means time or state. A relation of rest.

As Noah and his family found peace, rest, and safety, we have, and can find rest in Christ in this world, and confidence that the true ark will protect us.

"These things I have spoken unto you, that in me ye might have peace. In the world ye shall have tribulation: but be of good cheer; I have overcome the world." (John 16:33)

THE ONE DOOR

It is interesting that the ark Noah built had just one door, which was used both to enter and to leave.

We can relate this to what Jesus said:

"Jesus saith unto him, 'I am the way, the truth, and the life: no man cometh unto the Father, but by me.'" (John 14:6)

"Then said Jesus unto them again, 'Verily, verily, I say unto you, I am the door of the sheep.'" (John 10:7)

For through him we both have access by one Spirit unto the Father. Now therefore ye are no more strangers and foreigners, but fellow citizens with the saints, and of the household of God; And are built upon the foundation of the apostles and prophets, Jesus Christ himself being the chief corner stone; In whom all the building fitly framed together groweth unto an holy temple in the Lord: In whom ye also are builded together for an habitation (dwelling place) of God through the Spirit. (Eph. 2:18–22)

"Having therefore, brethren, boldness to enter into the holiest by the blood of Jesus." (Heb. 10:19)

God used examples, types, and shadows from the Bible to reveal what he would do through his Son. As you read your Bible, look for such types.

SALVATION IN THE ARK

To be saved (in Christ), we must first understand that when born into the world, we have Adam's sin of death passed onto us physically (Rom. 3:23–26, 6:23; 1 Cor. 15:22).

Our soul is covered in the womb by God's spirit until the day we sin (Ps. 139:13–16).

Consider the example of disobeying our parents, as one of those sins (Exod. 20:12; Eph. 6:3).

Once we sin, the Bible says we become dead in sin (Eph. 2:1–10), cursed, and condemned to the lake of fire (Matt. 25:41) because we no longer have God's spirit in our soul.

We need to know that we are not good enough to come to God by works of any kind. As a matter of fact, God sees everything we do as filthy rags (Isa. 59:2, 16; 64:6).

This takes repentance (changing the mind) to believe "Jesus" is the only way to God.

God loved us while we were yet sinners.

"But God commendeth (to set or bring together) his love toward us, in that, while we were yet sinners, Christ died for us" (Rom. 5:8).

God sent that love.

For God so loved the world, that he gave his only begotten Son, that whosoever believeth in him should not perish, but have everlasting life. For God sent not his Son into the world to condemn the world; but that the world through him might be saved. He that believeth on him is not condemned: but he that believeth not is condemned already, because he hath not believed in the name of the only begotten Son of God. (John 3:16–18)

We need to understand if we break God's laws, then we are dead in sin. After we sin, we must *pay for those sins* at the end of our life, because the wages of sin are death (Rom. 6:23) because God's spirit is no longer in us (Eph. 2:1–10). But there is good news. We need to understand that Jesus took our sins, paid for them, took the blame and shame on the cross to face punishment when he was innocent, and arose from the dead. *We need to receive him as our only debt payer* (2 Cor. 3:4–5, 5:21; Rom. 4:24–25, 5:2–4; Heb. 12:2, 4:16; Phil. 3:3; Eph. 3:11–12; Ps. 25:2).

We should confess (Greek: speak and same thing) as written by Paul:

> That if thou shalt confess with thy mouth the Lord Jesus, and shalt believe in thine heart that God hath raised him from the dead, thou shalt be saved. For with the heart man believeth unto righteousness; and with the mouth confession is made unto salvation. For the scripture saith, "Whosoever believeth on him shall not be ashamed." For there is no difference between the Jew and the Greek: for the same Lord over all is rich unto all that call upon him. For whosoever shall call upon the name of the Lord shall be saved. How then shall they call on him in whom they have not believed? and how shall they believe in him of whom they have not heard? and how shall they hear without a preacher? And how shall they preach, except they be sent? as it is written, How beautiful are the feet of them that preach the gospel of peace, and bring glad tidings of good things! But they have not all obeyed the gospel. For Esaias saith, "Lord, who hath believed our report?" So then faith cometh by hearing, and hearing by the word of God. (Rom. 10:9–17)

When we believe Jesus died and paid for our sins, the holy (separated) spirit of Christ Jesus enters into our spiritual soul, and we are "born again" (John 3:1–8).

Some feel differently after being "born again", while most do not, because this experience is spiritual, not physical. We can become emotional because the weight of the burdens seems to be less than it was before, while embracing the joy of our salvation. The experience of this is like the wind. Jesus gives examples in scripture about the wind (John 3:8).

We cannot see the wind, but we will see its effect around us. Our physical behavior will change by our free will by God's assistance as we work together in his spirit, learning and growing in his written Word, and speaking to him as we learn that biblical language.

God brought safety and soundness to Noah, and God shall be with us through Jesus Christ our Lord.

From inside of the ark, one can hear the storm. The ark of God was beaten by the waves of judgment while Noah and his family were safe and assisting the animals and walking by faith. Noah placed his trust in God, as should we, by faith. *Jesus our ark* was beaten by the storms of life, and our sins placed upon him. What he experienced brought us eternal life.

ALL ABOARD

God spoke to Noah to get into the Ark, before the destruction of the flood came: "For yet seven days, and I will cause it to rain upon the earth forty days and forty nights; and every living substance that I have made will I destroy from off the face of the earth. And Noah did according unto all that the Lord commanded him" (Gen. 7:4–5).

First Jesus speaks to us (through his written Word) to receive him, and to take him in. We become covered in Christ, as he covers our spiritual man, through salvation.

When Jesus came back from the dead, he spoke to his disciples to create more disciples and to spread the Word.

Jesus wants us to come to him before the terrible times come, not to face eternal judgment.

> And Jesus came and spake unto them, saying, "All power is given unto me in heaven and in earth. Go ye therefore, and teach (to be or make a disciple) all nations, baptizing them in the name of the Father, and of the Son, and of the Holy Ghost: Teaching them to observe all things whatsoever I have commanded you: and, lo, I am with you always, even unto the end of the world. Amen." (Matt. 28:18–20)

Jesus came first to the lost sheep of the house of Israel, and to the Jews. After his resurrection, he would tell his disciples *to go into all the world*. The apostle Paul continued this very idea:

> I am debtor both to the Greeks, and to the Barbarians; both to the wise, and to the unwise. So, as much as in me is, I am ready to preach the gospel to you that are at Rome also. For I am not ashamed of the gospel of Christ: for it is the power of God unto salvation to everyone that believeth; to the Jew first, and also to the Greek. (Rom. 1:14–16)

What is really awesome is that Jesus would pray for those in the future that would receive him, as he was praying for his disciples.

Look at this:

> Sanctify them through thy truth: thy word is truth. As thou hast sent me into the world, even so have I also sent them into the world. And for their sakes I sanctify myself, that they also might be sanctified through the truth. Neither pray I for these alone, but for them also which shall believe on me

through their word; That they all may be one; as thou, Father, art in me, and I in thee, that they also may be one in us: that the world may believe that thou hast sent me. And the glory which thou gavest me I have given them; that they may be one, even as we are one: I in them, and thou in me, that they may be made perfect in one; and that the world may know that thou hast sent me, and hast loved them, as thou hast loved me. (John 17:17–23)

Jesus "our ark" can be filled with more people; there is always room for another person.

They have that ticket to come aboard which was prepared for them by God the father. That ticket came at a great cost.

One day, the captain (Jesus, along with his angels) will blow the signal, and with a sound of the trumpet, the passengers will go up above the earth.

As Noah's ark was lifted up by the waves of the flood, so shall the church meet the *true ark in the clouds*. This is an example of when we meet the Lord in the air. This gives us an excellent example of our *deliverance in the Rapture*.

As God warned Noah, will he also let us know the storm is coming?

As is the earthy, such are they also that are earthy: and as is the heavenly, such are they also that are heavenly. And as we have borne the image of the earthy, we shall also bear the image of the heavenly. Now this I say, brethren, that flesh and blood cannot inherit the kingdom of God; neither doth corruption inherit incorruption. Behold, I shew you a mystery; We shall not all sleep, but we shall all be changed, In a moment, in the twinkling of an eye, at the last trump: for the trumpet shall sound, and the dead shall be raised incorruptible, and we shall be changed. For this corruptible must put on incorruption, and this mortal must put on immortality. So when this corruptible shall have put on incorruption, and this mortal shall have put on immortality, then shall be brought to pass the saying that is written, "Death is swallowed up in victory." (1 Cor. 15:48–54)

But I would not have you to be ignorant, brethren, concerning them which are asleep, that ye sorrow not, even as others which have no hope. For if we believe that Jesus died and rose again, even so them also which sleep in Jesus will God bring with him. For this we say unto you by the word of the Lord, that we which are alive and remain unto the coming of the Lord shall not prevent them which are asleep. For the Lord himself shall descend from heaven with a shout, with the voice of the archangel, and with the trump of God: and the dead in Christ shall rise first: Then we which are alive and remain shall be caught (snatched away) up together with them in the clouds, to meet the Lord in the air: and so shall we ever be with the Lord. Wherefore comfort one another with these words. (1 Thess. 4:13–18)

Millions of believers believe that Christ Jesus will come before the worse parts of the Tribulation occur upon the earth, just as the prophets, disciples, apostles, and Jesus spoke about.

I lean toward that teaching. Many teach Jesus comes in the clouds, and the dead in Christ are raised first, and we which are alive, will be changed, and will meet him in the air.

This event happens near the beginning of the seven-year Tribulation, in the period of false deceptive peace, and before this peace (deceptive peace) is taken from the earth.

This is based upon Paul's letters to the Thessalonians (1 Thess. 5:1–7, 9; 2 Thess. 2:1–3) and concerns things he learned from Jesus (Gal. 1:12; 1 Cor. 9:1; Eph. 3:3) and from what he read in Jeremiah 30:3–7. John confirms this peace (false deceptive peace by the man of sin) in Revelation 6:2, because in the next verses (3–4), the *peace is removed from the earth*, during the second seal. This is true future history written in symbolism.

The prophets and most disciples did not understand this until Jesus revealed it in detail first to Paul. There was *no church until after Jesus' resurrection*, and this would stay as a *mystery until it was revealed*.

The gathering together (the rapture) comes at a time of false peace and safety, according to Paul. Jeremiah 30 and John's letter (in Revelation 6:1–2) describe the deception of the *white horse of peace that conquers without arrows.*

Now look at this:

> But of the times and the seasons, brethren, ye have no need that I write unto you. For yourselves know perfectly that the day of the Lord so cometh as a thief in the night. For when they shall say, "Peace and safety"; then sudden destruction cometh upon them, as travail upon a woman with child; and they shall not escape. But ye, brethren, are not in darkness, that that day should overtake you as a thief. (1 Thess. 5:1–4)

Also:

> Now we beseech you, brethren, by the coming of our Lord Jesus Christ, and by our gathering together unto him, That ye be not soon shaken in mind, or be troubled, neither by spirit, nor by word, nor by letter as from us, as that the day of Christ is at hand. Let no man deceive you by any means: for that day

shall not come, except there come a falling away first, and that man of sin be revealed, the son of perdition. (2 Thess. 2:1–3)

Read both 1 and 2 Thessalonians together as one letter. The prophets understood that the *wrath was coming upon all the earth*, not just in that location of the Middle East. The wrath comes in the Day of God. That shows Jesus' second coming in vengeance (Isa. 61:1–2).

This is the *second advent*, spoken of by many pastors in the world. This event happens at the *end of the Great Tribulation*.

The Rapture takes place near the *beginning of the Tribulation* after a land covenant between Israel and some of the Arab states while there is peace on the earth.

The church will leave a little later, but *before the birth, pains become worse:* the trumpet shall sound the dead in Christ shall rise, and then we will be changed at the sound of the last trumpet, and go with our Lord into Heaven.

The falling away happens at the same time as this peace and safety.

Many will believe the *peace on the earth is from God*; however, it isn't; it's a deceptive political peace.

Those left behind (after the Rapture) will have another chance to receive Christ either by not accepting the *mark 666 on their right hand or forehead*, or by not receiving the beast's system: both of these choices involve their death after the middle of the seven-year Tribulation.

Jesus comes in all power near the end of the Great Tribulation, and the church will be with him. Yet he alone attacks the enemies, which are Satan's armies of the world that come against Israel.

Then Jesus will set up his kingdom for one thousand years with true peace.

Saints in Christ, there is so much more detail that this book could not possibly give you.

We all see through a glass darkly (1 Cor. 13:12) our understanding of God's Word, so we can only share what we know and understand. If you desire to study more on the Rapture and Jesus' second coming, please feel free to contact me on Facebook or my author's site, which will be provided at the end of this book.

Rescued

Jesus has provided this deliverance to rescue us, and not just to save us from the wrath to come, of which the prophets, Jesus, his disciples, and the apostles wrote. Jesus also gives us strength in tribulation and problems for our personal life, to bring salvation for our spirit and mind, and healing for our body. Many times, the word salvation in Greek, as well as in Hebrew, means safety, rest, and ease.

Jesus rescued us from bondage and corruption: "Because the creature itself also shall be delivered from the bondage of corruption into the glorious liberty of the children of God" (Rom. 8:21).

For healing and deliverance: "The Spirit of the Lord God is upon me; because the Lord hath anointed me to preach good tidings unto the meek; he hath sent me to bind up the brokenhearted, to proclaim liberty to the captives, and the opening of the prison to them that are bound" (Isa. 61:1).

"The Spirit of the Lord is upon me, because he hath anointed me to preach the gospel to the poor; he hath sent me to heal the brokenhearted, to preach deliverance to the captives, and recovering of sight to the blind, to set at liberty them that are bruised" (Luke 4:18).

Paul shared with the church that temptations will come, but God is steadfast not to allow us to be tempted above what we are able.

From our temptation of sin: "There hath no temptation taken you but such as is common to man: but God is faithful, who will not suffer you to be tempted above that ye are able (able to have power); but will with the temptation also make a way to escape that ye may be able to bear it" (1 Cor. 10:13).

For preaching his Word: "Persecutions, afflictions, which came unto me at Antioch, at Iconium, at Lystra; what persecutions I endured: but out of them all the Lord delivered me" (2 Tim. 3:11).

From death (until our time comes; Ps. 90:9–12): "Who delivered us from so great a death, and doth deliver: in whom we trust that he will yet deliver us" (2 Cor. 1:10).

From our fear (all types): "I sought the Lord, and he heard me, and delivered me from all my fears" (Ps. 34:4).

"For God hath not given us the spirit of fear; but of power, and of love, and of a sound mind" (2 Tim. 1:7).

From every evil work: "And the Lord shall deliver me from every evil work, and will preserve me unto his heavenly kingdom: to whom be glory for ever and ever. Amen" (2 Tim. 4:18).

From the powers of darkness: "Who hath delivered us from the power of darkness, and hath translated us into the kingdom of his dear Son" (Col. 1:13).

When we feel there is no one to help us: "Be not far from me; for trouble is near; for there is none to help" (Ps. 22:11).

Yet, God will be there if we call on him: "Then they cry unto the Lord in their trouble, and he saveth them out of their distresses" (Ps. 107:19).

For safety and protection, if we face the times of which the prophets, Jesus, Paul and Peter spoke:

But of the times and the seasons, brethren, ye have no need that I write unto you. For yourselves know perfectly that the day of the Lord so cometh as a thief in the night. For when they shall say, Peace and safety; then sudden destruction cometh upon them, as travail upon a woman with child; and they shall not escape. But ye, brethren, are not in darkness, that that day should overtake you as a thief. Ye are all the children of light, and the children of the day: we are not of the night, nor of darkness. Therefore let us not sleep, as do others; but let us watch and be sober. For they that sleep sleep in the night; and they that be drunken are drunken in the night. But let us, who are of the day, be sober, putting on the breastplate of faith and love; and for an helmet, the hope of salvation. For God hath not appointed us to wrath, but to obtain salvation by our Lord Jesus Christ. (1 Thess. 5:1–9)

The Lord Jesus has rescued us in so many ways, and as you read your Bible, learn from the examples and experiences of others so that you will understand more.

We all were dead in sin as Paul said (Eph. 2:1–10), facing judgment. Yet, God, in his mercy, sent his Son and brought salvation (John 3:16–18), and placed us in Jesus.

This is that *true ark of God* who will protect us before that flood of fire and destruction comes upon all the earth.

Our ark of safety and rest, Jesus.

THE COMING STORM

—⚏—

The earth was reeling to and fro like a drunkard (Isa. 24:20). The islands were moved (Rev. 6:14), great structures fell, and every wall was coming down (Matt. 24:2; Isa. 24:1–6, 13:13).

Giant cracks on the surface of the earth were swallowing massive numbers of people of unknown number in an abyss. Landmasses were crumbling as burnt logs on a fire. The waves of the sea crashing down upon the land were in competition with the burning landscape that was creating great cauldrons boiling any life that fell into it.

The skies were dark, the *sun became dark, and the moon became as blood* because of the *destruction upon the entire earth* (Rev. 6:12).

Screams of high-pitched terror were a common orchestra. Storms of fire and hail (Rev. 16:20–21; 2 Pet. 3:10) came upon the earth as the angels of God were blowing their trumpets and pouring out the wrath in the final days of the *Great Tribulation with Jesus' presence on the true white horse*, with a sharp sword coming out of his mouth (symbolism of the Word spoken by him, Rev. 19:15; Matt. 24:29).

The world will be in the *same condition* as before the flood according to Matthew's Gospel spoken by Jesus:

> But as the days of Noah were, so shall also the coming of the Son of man be. For as in the days that were before the flood they were eating and drinking, marrying and giving in marriage, until the day that Noe entered into the ark, And knew not until the flood came, and took them all away; so shall also the coming of the Son of man be. (Matt. 24:37–39)

This is clear by the words of Matthew spoken in the spirit by our Lord Jesus.

When we think of a storm, we think of clouds, wind, and rain, and of what the storm brings. We can observe the damage of tornadoes, and their violent rotating damage along with large hail and high wind. Hurricanes include powerful winds, heavy rainfall, storm surges, coastal and inland flooding, rip currents, tornadoes, and landslides.

This gives us somewhat an idea of what happened when Noah's flood came.

From what we studied in Noah's days and of Cain's descendants, both before and after the flood, the same scheme was accomplished with a city and tower, as *built by Nimrod*.

Satan would use "*peace and safety*" to draw his plans of deceit: *a world peace of unity and economic prosperity.* This false peace was a plan for world unity, even though the peace would not last because it was not God's peace. It was only a deception to seduce man by the desires within him. God warned through the prophets of such days coming.

One example was through Daniel's writings by an angel that told him:

> And in the latter time of their kingdom, when the transgressors are come to the full, a king of fierce countenance, and understanding dark sentences, shall stand up. And his power shall be mighty, but not by his own power: and he shall destroy wonderfully,

and shall prosper, and practise, and shall destroy the mighty and the holy people. And through his policy also he shall cause craft to prosper in his hand; and he shall magnify himself in his heart, and by peace shall destroy many: he shall also stand up against the Prince of princes; but he shall be broken without hand. (Dan. 8:23–25)

If you notice in verse 25, he says by peace he shall destroy (Hebrew: corrupt). Not all people, but many people, view this person to be the man of sin, *known as the Antichrist,* of whom is spoken in the New Testament. You need to read the entire book of Daniel carefully.

Keep in mind either that this was fulfilled in the past, is happening now, or is for the future, or else it is all symbolic. People have many different views on these teachings.

If we allow the scriptures to teach us, I believe we will find the answer. Do not take anyone's word; study it for yourself. We read that Paul spoke about a *time of false peace coming* (1 Thess. 5:1–3).

Jesus even gave us clues in Matthew:

And as he sat upon the mount of Olives, the disciples came unto him privately, saying, "Tell us, when shall these things be? and what shall be the sign of thy coming, and of the end of the world (age)?" And Jesus answered and said unto them, "Take heed that no man deceive you. For many shall come in my name, saying, 'I am Christ;' and shall deceive many." (Matt. 24:3–5)

Now for some details.

What is his name? His name is Jesus, Yahusha, Yahshua, Yeshuah and known as "savior" in Greek.

In Greek, Jesus' name means savior. The word "Jesus" is the Latin form of the Greek "*Iesous*", which in turn is a transliteration of the Hebrew *Jeshua*, *Jahusha*, Joshua, or Jehoshua, meaning "Jehovah is Salvation."

Joshua means "Yahweh is salvation", if we use the proper Hebrew name of God. Jehovah is salvation. From Strong's Concordance, Jesus = "Jehovah is salvation", an English translation.

God is called *Yah* in Hebrew, and *Shua* in Hebrew means savior. You then have the name Yah-shua, God and savior.

Joshua: יְהוֹשׁוּעַ Yĕhowshuwa` — yeh·hō·shü'·ah (pronunciation, according to the Strong's Hebrew).

Joshua = Yoshua or Yeshua, because there is no "J" sound in Hebrew. The letter "J" is only about five hundred years old.

Also in Hebrew: Yeshua HaMashiach

In Greek, "Christ" means anointed. Christos, Christ, was (and is) the Messiah, the Son of God.

In Hebrew, Messiah, *Mashiyach*, means anointed, anointed one, of the Messiah, Messianic prince (Dan. 9:25–26) of the king of Israel, the high priest of Israel.

Along with other kings that ruled over Israel, the high priest in the Old Testament was anointed with oil. Jesus would be "*the Anointed*" of God (Acts 10:38; Matt. 3:16–17).

We know many that claim that they are Jesus Christ in strange religions of the past and of today, or they say they are the Christ.

Matthew 24:5, in the words of Jesus, it is written, "For many shall come in my name."

They are coming in his name, *saying that they are anointed*. This verse is not saying that these people are claiming to be Jesus Christ, but rather that they are coming in his name and they and claiming that they are anointed.

The Bible warns of a *falling away, and of peace and safety* happening at the same time.

The deception is the false peace coming by this man (claiming to be anointed), and by the many others in verse 5.

Who are they?

They are saying that they are anointed by God, and this is a lie.

These others are revealed in Revelation and are known as the beast (Antichrist, man of sin, his seven heads) that are religious leaders of the world and on their heads the names of blasphemy and the ten crowns (which are ten kings' crowns on the heads; Rev. 13:1), another beast that speaks like a lamb (false prophet; Rev. 13:11–13), and the image created by hands that comes to life (Rev. 13:12–15). They are also referred to in Revelation 16:13–14:

> And I saw three unclean spirits like frogs come out of the mouth of the dragon, and out of the mouth of the beast, and out of the mouth of the false prophet. For they are the spirits of devils, working miracles, which go forth unto the kings of the earth and of the whole world, to gather them to the battle of that great day of God Almighty.

The Bible was written literally and symbolically, and as we read the context and precepts, we can learn the difference.

The details are amazing all throughout God's Word. This is the main reason God told people not to worship graven images (Exod. 20:1–5). Yehweh knew what was coming in the future.

An image comes to life, and Satan (who is a spirit) enters into it. He declares himself as God, and God allows this.

The abomination that brings the desolation fulfills his time in the middle of the seven-year tribulation, and he brings to pass the prophecies that the prophets wrote about in the Bible concerning this evil.

As you read the Bible in the books by Daniel and John (who wrote Revelation), both of these men of God uncovered the abomination, as did other writers in the Bible.

To understand the book of Revelation, you must read and study Daniel along with Revelation. This includes reading Paul's letters and the Gospels where they speak of these same events. These events will be heard because of this false peace of which Jeremiah speaks:

> And these are the words that the Lord spake concerning Israel and concerning Judah. For thus saith the Lord; "We have heard a voice of trembling, of fear, and not of peace. Ask ye now, and see whether a man doth travail with child? wherefore do I see every man with his hands on his loins, as a woman in travail, and all faces are turned into paleness? Alas! for that day is great, so that none is like it: it is even the time of Jacob's trouble, but he shall be saved out of it." (Jer. 30:4–7)

> And ye shall hear of wars and rumours of wars: see that ye be not troubled: for all these things must come to pass, but the end is not yet. For nation shall rise against nation, and kingdom against kingdom: and there shall be famines, and pestilences, and earthquakes, in divers places. All these are the beginning of sorrows (birth pains). (Matt. 24:6–8)

The Bible says there will be a major war involving Israel, after which there will be peace.

The man of sin is a *political leader who will bring peace* (deceptive world peace), and then will *confirm a land covenant.* Israel will regain more land after that war for their own safety, since it is God's design to bring them into the land, according to Jeremiah 30:1–3 that they possessed under Moses and Joshua.

Some will agree with this, and some will not. As I said previously, there are different interpretations in our churches because of different backgrounds and prejudices on how we were taught or were not taught, and this makes it a big challenge when discussing this topic.

Isn't it worthwhile and valuable to take more time to study God's Word and to benefit from it by many other things as you learn?

Many of us have different beliefs on the Rapture, the second coming of Christ, and Bible prophecy, whether fulfilled, semi-fulfilled, or not fulfilled. If we are heading toward *"the days of Noah"*, will God show us the same mercy as he showed Noah and his family? Will there be events to know that the "rain" is coming?

The world will face this storm, a storm not of rain, but of a Middle East War, that will spread involving other major powers, and then of a false peace (set up by the man of sin) which will cover the whole earth. This will start the birth pains once the land-covenant is fulfilled.

The church will be caught up (which caught up is known by many as the rapture) and then we shall be with the Lord during the time of false peace and safety that is on the earth then it gets bad for those who are left behind.

The church (those born again) will not go into the *wrath of the Great Tribulation.*

Different levels of destruction for the remainder of the seven years will be on the earth as Jesus opens the seals and releases his angels.

Then after the seven-year Tribulation, the Messiah will come with his church to set up his reign on earth, just as Noah's ark rested after the flood.

Spiritual warfare requires that one have on the *whole armor of God daily* (in the mind, according to Eph. 6:10–18), walking with him in prayer, studying his written Word (2 Tim. 2:15), and helping those in need when it's in our power to do so.

We need to be watchful and awake in the times we are living. We need to study his Word daily to *discern between good and evil* (Deut. 17:18–20). We need to help ourselves, our children, and our friends and acquaintances by ministering the truth. We need to be at *peace and rest* no matter what comes our way.

"Submit to God, resist the devil and he will flee from you" (James 4:7).

Jesus also said not to be over anxious about tomorrow: "Take therefore no thought (to be anxious) for the morrow: for the morrow shall take thought for the things of itself. Sufficient unto the day is the evil thereof" (Matt. 6:34).

Take each day as a gift and use it wisely, seeking after God through Jesus Christ our Lord and Savior, sharing what he did for you, and what is coming on the earth, so that those who don't believe might consider getting into the ark before the storm comes.

God bless you in the power, wisdom, strength and love of Jesus Christ our Lord.

BIBLIOGRAPHY

—ɯ—

Pangaea page 10 https://en.wikipedia.org/wiki/Pangaea

Continental drift page 11 https://en.wikipedia.org/wiki/Continental_drift

Liberal page 19 https://en.oxforddictionaries.com/definition/liberal

City page 20 https://www.britannica.com/topic/city

Atlantis page 23 https://en.wikipedia.org/wiki/Atlantis

Iron page 26 https://en.wikipedia.org/wiki/I

Tubal-cain page 27 (https://en.wikipedia.org/wiki/Tubal-cain)

Solar rays, Sunlight page 37 https://en.wikipedia.org/wiki/Sunlight

Dinosaur page 38 https://en.wikipedia.org/wiki/Dinosaur

Worship page 41 https://www.merriam-webster.com/dictionary/worship

Book of Enoch page 62 https://en.wikipedia.org/wiki/Book_of_Enoch

Male or female by the proof of genetics page 82 From https://www.
google.com/search?q=male+and+female+by+Genneics&rlz=1C-
1CHBF_enUS776US776&oq=male+and+female+by+Genne-
ics&aqs=chrome..69i57j33.18825j1j4&sourceid=chrome&ie=UTF-8

Suicide page 87 https://www.google.com/search?q=Sui-
cide+is+the+2nd+leading&rlz=1C1CHBF_enUS776US776&oq=Sui-

cide+is+the+2nd+leading&aqs=chrome..69i57j0.3687j0j9&sourceid=-
chrome&ie=UTF-8

Narcissistic page 77 https://www.merriam-webster.com/dictionary/
narcissistic

Gluttony page 108 https://en.wikipedia.org/wiki/Gluttony

Idleness page 124 https://www.dictionary.com/browse/idleness

—⁓—

Here are my sites. Hope to see you.

https://www.facebook.com/wechandler1948/ (Author site)

https://www.facebook.com/william.chandler.357 Facebook.

You can purchase other books written by
William E. Chandler:

Beyond Paradise: the Story of our Ultimate Redemption

The Lord's Prayer Unveiled: Reflections from the Mount

Put on the Whole Armor of God: A Believer's Warfare

Spiritual Warfare: The Battle Continues